Euthanasia

[OPPOSING
VIEWPOINTS®
DIGESTS]

Euthanasia

JAMES D. TORR

Greenhaven Press, Inc., San Diego, California

Library of Congress Cataloging-in-Publication Data

Torr, James D., 1974
   Euthanasia / by James D. Torr.
      p.   cm. — (Opposing viewpoints digests)
   Includes bibliographical references and index.
   Summary: Presents opposing arguments on the debate concerning euthanasia, including ethical issues, physician participation, and the legalization of voluntary euthanasia.
      ISBN 1-56510-870-1 (pbk. : alk. paper). — ISBN 1-56510-871-X (lib. : alk. paper)

98-42321
CIP
AC

Cover Photo: © Tony Stone Images/Terry Vine
Archive Photos: 18
Photo Researchers: 35
Reuters/Rebecca Cook/Archive Photos: 88

©1999 by Greenhaven Press, Inc.
PO Box 289009, San Diego, CA 92198-9009

Printed in the U.S.A.

CONTENTS

FOREWORD

The only way in which a human being can make some approach to knowing the whole of a subject is by hearing what can be said about it by persons of every variety of opinion and studying all modes in which it can be looked at by every character of mind. No wise man ever acquired his wisdom in any mode but this.

—John Stuart Mill

Today, young adults are inundated with a wide variety of points of view on an equally wide spectrum of subjects. Often overshadowing traditional books and newspapers as forums for these views are a host of broadcast, print, and electronic media, including television news and entertainment programs, talk shows, and commercials; radio talk shows and call-in lines; movies, home videos, and compact discs; magazines and supermarket tabloids; and the increasingly popular and influential Internet.

For teenagers, this multiplicity of sources, ideas, and opinions can be both positive and negative. On the one hand, a wealth of useful, interesting, and enlightening information is readily available virtually at their fingertips, underscoring the need for teens to recognize and consider a wide range of views besides their own. As Mark Twain put it, "It were not best that we should all think alike; it is difference of opinion that makes horse races." On the other hand, the range of opinions on a given subject is often too wide to absorb and analyze easily. Trying to keep up with, sort out, and form personal opinions from such a barrage can be daunting for anyone, let alone young people who have not yet acquired effective critical judgment skills.

Moreover, to the task of evaluating this assortment of impersonal information, many teenagers bring firsthand experience of serious and emotionally charged social and health problems, including divorce, family violence, alcoholism and drug abuse, rape, unwanted pregnancy, the spread of AIDS, and eating disorders. Teens are often forced to deal with these problems before they are capable of objective opinion based on reason and judgment. All too often, teens' response to these deep personal issues is impulsive rather than carefully considered.

Greenhaven Press's Opposing Viewpoints Digests are designed to aid in examining important current issues in a way that develops critical thinking and evaluating skills. Each book presents thought-provoking argument and stimulating debate on a single issue. By examining an issue from many different points of view, readers come to realize its complexity and acknowledge the validity of opposing opinions. This insight is especially helpful in writing reports, research papers, and persuasive essays, when students must competently address common objections and controversies related to their topic. In addition, examination of the diverse mix of opinions in each volume challenges readers to question their own strongly held opinions and assumptions. While the point of such examination is not to change readers' minds, examining views that oppose their own will certainly deepen their own knowledge of the issue and help them realize exactly why they hold the opinion they do.

The Opposing Viewpoints Digests offer a number of unique features that sharpen young readers' critical thinking and reading skills. To assure an appropriate and consistent reading level for young adults, all essays in each volume are written by a single author. Each essay heavily quotes readable primary sources that are fully cited to allow for further research and documentation. Thus, primary sources are introduced in a context to enhance comprehension.

In addition, each volume includes extensive research tools. A section containing relevant source material includes interviews, excerpts from original research, and the opinions of prominent spokespersons. A "facts about" section allows students to peruse relevant facts and statistics; these statistics are also fully cited, allowing students to question and analyze the credibility of the source. Two bibliographies, one for young adults and one listing the author's sources, are also included; both are annotated to guide student research. Finally, a comprehensive index allows students to scan and locate content efficiently.

Greenhaven's Opposing Viewpoints Digests, like Greenhaven's higher level and critically acclaimed Opposing Viewpoints Series, have been developed around the concept that an awareness and appreciation for the complexity of seemingly simple issues is particularly important in a democratic society. In a democracy, the common good is often, and very appropriately, decided by open debate of widely varying views. As one of our democracy's greatest advocates, Thomas Jefferson, observed, "Difference of opinion leads to inquiry, and inquiry to truth." It is to this principle that Opposing Viewpoints Digests are dedicated.

"Distinguishing between the various types of euthanasia is important in understanding the complexities of the issue."

The Euthanasia Debate Today

Euthanasia is the act of killing or permitting the death of hopelessly sick or injured individuals in a relatively painless way for reasons of mercy. Supporters of euthanasia feel that ending a person's life can be justifiable if the person is in severe pain and sincerely wants to die. They maintain that euthanasia is sometimes the only way to relieve extreme suffering. Opponents of euthanasia, on the other hand, contend that killing and suicide are always wrong. The euthanasia debate reflects a moral dilemma between those who feel that ending suffering should take priority over preserving life and those who believe that mercy killing and suicide can never be justified.

Ancient Origins

People have always feared a painful, lingering death, and the debate over euthanasia is as ancient as this fear. The word *euthanasia* comes from the Greek phrase meaning "good death." It is derived from *eu*, meaning "good," and *thanatos*, meaning "death." Because so much of modern law and philosophy is rooted in Greek and Roman antiquity, both sides of the euthanasia debate have been interested in how these societies regarded mercy killing.

In modern discussions of euthanasia, physician-assisted suicide (in which a doctor supplies lethal pills to a patient, who must then choose whether to take them) is the most prominently featured form, and many scholars believe that the Greeks supported rational, planned suicide as a way to achieve a "good death." In certain areas of the Greek realm, it may have been customary for people over age sixty to kill themselves by drinking a cup of the poison hemlock. One author notes that "in Western literature, the term 'drink the cup of Hemlock' has, through Shakespeare and others, come to mean the way to rational suicide."[1] Seneca, the Roman philosopher and statesman, "recommended suicide when old age threatened to bring undignified decay,"[2] according to Anton Van Hoof, author of *From Autothanasia to Suicide: Self-Killing in Classical Antiquity*.

Yet there is also evidence that the ancient Greeks opposed suicide and euthanasia, even in cases of unbearable suffering. Some findings indicate that people who committed suicide were not honored in celebrations for the dead. The most often cited evidence that the Greeks opposed euthanasia, however, is the Hippocratic oath, which is named for the famous physician Hippocrates, later dubbed "the Father of Medicine." The Hippocratic oath enjoins doctors never to "give a deadly drug to anybody if asked for it, nor . . . make a suggestion to this effect."[3] Classical Greek physicians swore to follow the rules proscribed in the oath, and many doctors today believe its ancient prohibition on physician-assisted suicide should be respected.

Clearly, opinion about euthanasia varied in ancient times, and the decision to kill oneself, or to be killed, has remained a controversial topic throughout history. With the rise of Christianity, many people adopted the belief that life is a gift from God. Suicide came to be viewed as a gravely immoral act because it was a rejection of this gift. However, during the Enlightenment in the eighteenth century, many philosophers began to criticize the teachings of the church as irrational and oppressive. Famous Enlightenment thinkers such as Voltaire argued that suicide could be both rational and moral. Although the term *euthanasia* was not used, these arguments for rational suicide were often based on the idea that people with life-threatening diseases may have good reasons to want to die.

The Modern Euthanasia Debate

Suicide has always been a contentious issue, but it is only in the twentieth century that governments have been forced to confront the issue of euthanasia. In his book *Hemlock's Cup: The Struggle for Death with Dignity*, Donald Cox states that the modern right-to-die movement can be traced back to 1935, when "a group of intellectual mavericks, headed by George Bernard Shaw, Harold Lanski, Bertrand Russell, and H.G. Wells, founded the British Euthanasia Society."[4] This was the first of several movements in various nations to advocate legalizing euthanasia. World War II put a temporary halt to these movements, however, and the euthanasia debate did not resurface in America until the 1970s.

The euthanasia debate took on a renewed urgency in the 1970s partly because Americans were living longer. Average life expectancy in America had jumped from forty-seven years in 1900 to seventy-one in 1970. Medical technology had advanced incredibly rapidly since World War II, and doctors were becoming increasingly skilled at keeping people alive who would certainly have died in an earlier era. There was growing tension between doctors' zeal to preserve life and patients' desire for a peaceful death. This tension culminated in the 1976 court case of Karen Ann Quinlan, the first euthanasia case to come before a U.S. court.

In 1975, after consuming alcohol and tranquilizers at a party, Quinlan collapsed into an irreversible coma that left her unable to breathe without a respirator or eat without a feeding tube. Her parents asked that she be removed from the respirator, but her doctors objected. In a landmark decision, the New Jersey Supreme Court allowed Quinlan's parents to have the respirator removed. The court's reasoning was that patients (or family members acting on their behalf) have the right to refuse any medical treatment they deem inappropriate, even if the treatment is necessary to prolong life. This decision was controversial because it challenged the idea that

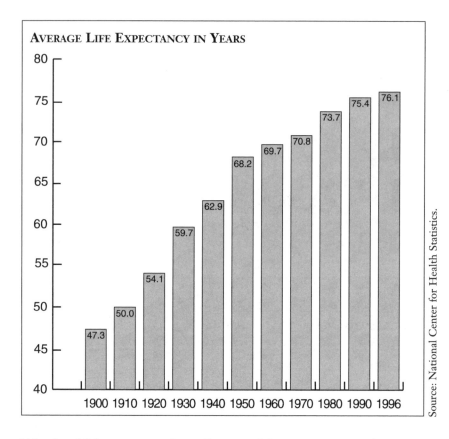

AVERAGE LIFE EXPECTANCY IN YEARS

Source: National Center for Health Statistics.

life should be preserved at all costs. Moreover, it set the stage for discussion of other forms of euthanasia, besides "pulling the plug" on artificial respirators.

"It's Over, Debbie"

By the 1980s most Americans accepted that patients should not be hooked up to lifesaving machines against their will, and other types of euthanasia became the focus of attention. In 1988 the *Journal of the American Medical Association* unleashed a storm of controversy when it published a short article submitted by an anonymous medical resident. In the article, the physician-in-training describes how he performed euthanasia on a twenty-year-old woman named Debbie who was dying of ovarian cancer. He explains how he found Debbie exhausted and emaciated from having been unable to sleep in over two days. She simply said, "Let's get this over with," and he then injected her with enough morphine to stop her breathing. The anonymous author ended the article with the words, "It's over, Debbie."[5]

The cases of Debbie and Karen Ann Quinlan both involved the same difficult choice: whether the patient's quality of life was so intolerably low that death would be a blessing. Yet, for a variety of reasons, their cases were very different. The removal of Karen Ann Quinlan's respirator was done legally and only after serious consideration over whether it was morally the correct thing to do. In contrast, the anonymous medical resident acted on impulse, ending the life of a patient he knew little about without taking the time to assess the patient's mental state or to discuss the alternatives. Most importantly, his act was illegal because he killed Debbie with a lethal injection rather than allowing her to die of natural causes. The two cases involve very different methods of hastening death, and distinguishing between the various types of euthanasia is important in understanding the complexities of the issue.

Voluntary vs. Involuntary

The first distinction to make when discussing euthanasia is between voluntary and involuntary euthanasia. Simply put, voluntary euthanasia is performed at the patient's request, whereas involuntary euthanasia occurs without a patient's explicit consent or even against his or her will. This distinction is of utmost importance: A mercy killing that occurs without the explicit request of the patient is a form of homicide.

While few individuals openly advocate involuntary euthanasia, Americans are increasingly divided over whether it might be ethical if the patient requests it. Thus, the current debate over euthanasia is really a debate over voluntary euthanasia. During discussions of euthanasia, authors will sometimes omit the word *voluntary*. This is usually because they find it redundant: They feel that what separates euthanasia from homicide is that euthanasia is, by definition, voluntary.

In the case of comatose patients like Karen Ann Quinlan, the line between voluntary and involuntary euthanasia is blurred. In these situations, the courts have ruled that family members may sometimes act on the patient's behalf. The specific rules regarding who may make such decisions are complex and vary from state to state. Many patients choose to sign advance directives in which they designate a specific person, such as a friend or family member, to act as a surrogate decision maker should they become incompetent. Others make a living will, explaining in advance their wishes regarding euthanasia. But the principle remains the same: For euthanasia to be permissible, there must be evidence that the patient would have desired it.

Passive vs. Active Euthanasia

Several different voluntary euthanasia methods are commonly discussed:

- The first is the removal of life-support systems for a patient in an irreversible coma. These patients, such as Karen Ann Quinlan, are usually considered "brain dead" already, and this type of euthanasia is no longer very controversial, although some people remain opposed to it.
- The second is withholding treatment that may prolong, but not cure, a severely ill patient. For example, doctors might not perform cardiopulmonary resuscitation (CPR) on a heart attack victim who is already hopelessly ill. Patients may tell doctors to do exactly this by signing "do not resuscitate" orders.
- The third is direct, active euthanasia, in which a doctor administers a lethal injection at the patient's request. This is the type of euthanasia that the anonymous medical resident performed on Debbie.
- The final method is physician-assisted suicide, in which a doctor gives a patient the means to kill himself or herself.

The first two methods are often referred to as forms of passive euthanasia. They are considered passive because the doctor does not do anything to intentionally cause death. The doctor in the first case simply ceases treatment and allows the coma to run its course; in the second case, the doctor refrains from treatment and allows death to occur.

Although there is no longer much debate about passive euthanasia, some people remain opposed to it and contend that life should be preserved at all costs. Passive euthanasia has been legal since the case of Karen Ann Quinlan, because the courts have recognized the right of a patient (or a patient's surrogate) to refuse or to terminate unwanted medical treatments. The question that remains today is whether the last two types of euthanasia—physician-assisted suicide and active, voluntary euthanasia—should also be legalized.

Physician-Assisted Suicide vs. Active Euthanasia

The euthanasia debate is largely about the ethical question of whether the immorality of killing outweighs the duty to respect patients' wishes and to relieve needless suffering. However, much of the opposition to euthanasia is rooted in practical, not ethical, concerns. Some opponents of active euthanasia do not oppose it morally but worry that if doctors have the power to kill patients, they may use it too freely. Thus, much of the opposition to active, voluntary euthanasia comes from the fear that, if it is legalized, it will be abused. For example, many people express concern that the anonymous physician-in-training so easily acceded to Debbie's request for euthanasia. They worry that doctors like him might be too willing to euthanize patients even when they do not explicitly request it—thus crossing the line into involuntary euthanasia and murder. Because of these fears, most right-to-die advocates support physician-assisted suicide rather than active, voluntary euthanasia.

Advocates of physician-assisted suicide insist that it is inherently voluntary. The doctor prescribes the lethal medication, but the patient must choose to swallow the pills. Thus, they contend, the patient retains control over the entire process. The advantages of physician-assisted suicide, as opposed to active euthanasia, were articulated by Dr. Timothy E. Quill in a 1991 *New England Journal of Medicine* article. Quill described the case of Diane, a longtime patient of his who was suffering from acute leukemia. She asked Quill for the means to end her life should she find it intolerable, and, unable to dissuade her, he prescribed sleeping pills, telling her how many were necessary to cure insomnia and how many were necessary to commit suicide. Four months later Diane killed herself.

Since the publication of Quill's article, physician-assisted suicide has been the most talked about form of euthanasia. Many proponents consider physician-assisted suicide to give power over death to the patient, not the doctor. As Quill explains, "The balance of power between doctor and patient is more nearly equal in physician-assisted suicide. The physician is counselor and witness, and makes the means available, but ultimately the patient must act or not act on his own."[6] But physician-assisted suicide is also more accepted than active euthanasia because it involves suicide rather than killing. For whatever reason, many people consider suicide less morally objectionable than euthanasia. According to Dr. Jerome P. Kassirer, "Assisting suicide by supplying the necessary drugs is considered somewhere in between [letting die and killing], more active than switching off a ventilator but less active than injecting drugs, hence morally and legally more ambiguous."[7]

In the eyes of opponents, however, physician-assisted suicide is not morally superior to active, voluntary euthanasia. Although one involves suicide rather than killing, in both types of euthanasia the doctor helps to bring about the death of the patient. Opponents believe that the self-killing of assisted suicide is just as wrong as the mercy killing of active euthanasia. In addition, euthanasia opponents distrust the claim that physician-assisted suicide is not prone to abuse, and they contend that legalization of assisted suicide is merely the first step toward legalization of active euthanasia.

The Right-to-Die Movement Gains National Publicity

While the medical community debated the cases of Debbie and Diane, popular support for euthanasia was growing. In 1991, the same year that Quill published his article, Derek Humphry published *Final Exit: The Practicalities of Self-Deliverance and Assisted Suicide for the Dying*. Essentially a how-to manual on euthanasia and physician-assisted suicide, *Final Exit* taught people the most effective ways to quickly and painlessly end life—knowledge that many people feel should be reserved for physicians. Nevertheless, the book became a surprise success, selling over half a million copies and spending eighteen weeks on the *New York Times* best-seller list. Humphry had founded the Hemlock Society, a right-to-die group named for the Greek poison, a decade earlier, but it was the phenomenal success of *Final Exit* that proved that large numbers of Americans were interested in assisted suicide and euthanasia.

Also around this time, retired pathologist Jack Kevorkian became infamous for assisting patients in committing suicide. "Doctor Death," as he was soon dubbed, helped Janet Adkins, a fifty-four-year-old woman with Alzheimer's disease, commit suicide in 1990. Adkins was the first of dozens of patients that Kevorkian would help to die during the 1990s. He has been charged with murder, and subsequently acquitted, several times. Kevorkian uses the term *medicide* to describe his method of assisting in suicide, and in his book *Prescription Medicide: The Goodness of Planned Death*, he makes several proposals that are entirely out of step with the mainstream right-to-die movement, including the idea that experiments should be conducted on death-row prison inmates before they are executed. Kevorkian's exploits made him famous, but his bizarre views left many people ambivalent about the ethics of physician-assisted suicide. Nevertheless, it is Jack Kevorkian, more than any other person, who is most responsible for drawing media attention to the right-to-die movement.

Jack Kevorkian has helped over one hundred patients commit suicide. He compares his intentions in helping suffering people end their lives to those of an executioner who upholds the law.

Physician-Assisted Suicide Is Legalized in Oregon

In an effort to capitalize on the growing popular support for physician-assisted suicide, right-to-die advocates in several states attempted to pass legislation that would allow doctors to grant requests for assistance in suicide. Voter referenda to legalize physician-assisted suicide in Washington State and California failed in the early 1990s, and a similar law failed to pass in Kevorkian's home state of Michigan in 1998. However, in 1994 Oregon voters passed Measure 16, which made the Oregon Death with Dignity Act into law. It was held up in legal wrangling for years, but the law finally went into effect in October 1997, making Oregon the only place in the world where physician-assisted suicide is legal. (Assisted suicide was briefly legalized in Australia's Northern Territory from July 1996 to March 1997. Although both physician-assisted suicide and active, voluntary euthanasia are accepted practices in the Netherlands, they remain technically illegal.)

The Supreme Court Rejects a Constitutional Right to Die

Voters in most states, however, have been reluctant to even consider legalizing physician-assisted suicide, indicating that popular support for euthanasia is not as strong as advocates had hoped. So, after voters rejected a 1991 ballot measure to legalize physician-assisted suicide in Washington State, right-to-die activists there tried a different tactic. They filed a lawsuit against the state, claiming that Washington's ban on assisted suicide violated the constitutional rights of terminally ill patients. Right-to-die activists in New York State made a similar claim shortly thereafter. In 1996 two federal courts ruled that the New York and Washington laws were unconstitutional—that is, they ruled that Americans have a constitutional right to physician-assisted suicide. Obviously, these rulings were heralded as major victories by supporters of euthanasia.

However, in early 1997 the Supreme Court overturned both of the lower courts' decisions. Although the Supreme Court did not rule that physician-assisted suicide was unconstitutional, it stated that the Constitution does not guarantee individuals a right to physician-assisted suicide or to euthanasia; the states must decide the issue for themselves.

Although suicide and euthanasia are ancient moral dilemmas, the modern debate over physician-assisted dying is a relatively recent phenomenon. Less than thirty years passed between the nation's first case of passive euthanasia and the Supreme Court's decision on physician-assisted suicide. In that time, progress has been made in understanding a patient's legal right to passive euthanasia, but the broader questions remain: Is it morally acceptable to kill a person in order to relieve his or her suffering? Should it be legally permissible to help a person die if the person requests it? Americans have yet to reach a consensus on what the answer to these age-old questions should be, and euthanasia remains, for most, a moral dilemma.

1. Donald W. Cox, *Hemlock's Cup: The Struggle for Death with Dignity.* Amherst, NY: Prometheus Books, 1993, p. 59.

2. Quoted in Michael Herman, "Assisted Suicide: A History," *Journal of the Hippocratic Society,* Fall 1997, p. 46.

3. Quoted in Leon R. Kass and Nelson Lund, "Courting Death: Assisted Suicide, Doctors, and the Law," *Commentary,* December 1996, p. 19.

4. Cox, *Hemlock's Cup,* p. 23.

5. Quoted in Michael M. Uhlmann, ed., *Last Rights?: Assisted Suicide and Euthanasia Debated.* Grand Rapids, MI: William B. Eerdmans, 1998, p. 318.

6. Timothy E. Quill, *Death and Dignity: Making Choices and Taking Charge.* New York: W.W. Norton, 1993, p. 159.

7. Jerome P. Kassirer, "The Supreme Court and Physician-Assisted Suicide—the Ultimate Right," *New England Journal of Medicine,* January 2, 1997, p. 50.

CHAPTER 1

Is Euthanasia Ethical?

"Many terminally ill patients feel that their life has already been destroyed by disease—euthanasia only hastens their already imminent death."

Euthanasia Is Ethical

In his book *A Chosen Death: The Dying Confront Assisted Suicide*, Lonny Shavelson tells the story of Renee Sahm and her long fight against brain cancer. For over four years Renee explored new and experimental treatments and underwent brain surgery twice, determined to beat the disease. Unfortunately, her tumor returned again and again, finally spreading to the lymph gland in her neck. This made it difficult for her to swallow—she became chronically dehydrated and over the course of many months became weaker, while her pain grew worse.

In the several years that she lived with her illness, Renee had thought about how she wished to die, but she was determined to fight her cancer as long as she could. However, after five years of fighting, Renee was bedridden, emaciated, and unable to eat or drink. She was in great pain, which could only be relieved by medications that often made her groggy and incoherent, and her doctors saw no hope for recovery. Finally Renee decided that she wanted to die. But ironically, because she had held out against the disease for so long, she was now too weak to take her own life. Renee needed assistance in dying.

She was fortunate enough to have several friends who had cared for her throughout her illness and who respected her wishes regarding euthanasia. They procured for her a large dose of morphine. Renee administered it herself. It quickly put her to sleep, then slowly suppressed her breathing, finally stopping it completely. She died a calm, peaceful death, surrounded by people who cared for her.

Criteria for Justifiable Euthanasia

Technically, Renee committed suicide. But because she needed help, her death was an assisted suicide—a form of euthanasia. Derek Humphry, founder of the national right-to-die group the Hemlock Society, describes euthanasia as "rational and planned self-deliverance from a painful and hopeless disease which will shortly end in death."[1] Renee's case certainly fits this description.

In helping her to die, Renee's friends performed an act of caring and compassion. Euthanasia was the ethical choice because Renee met the following three criteria: Her quality of life had diminished to the point that she was experiencing intolerable suffering, she had no hope of recovery, and she expressed a sincere desire for assistance in dying. In his book *Death and Dignity: Making Choices and Taking Charge*, Dr. Timothy E. Quill describes several other types of patients who meet the criteria for justifiable euthanasia:

> A former athlete, weighing eighty pounds after an eight-year struggle with [AIDS], who is losing his sight and his memory and is terrified of AIDS dementia.

> A mother of seven children, continually exhausted and bedridden at home with a gaping, foul-smelling, open wound in her abdomen, who can no longer eat, and who no longer finds any meaning in her fight against ovarian cancer.

> A fiercely independent retired factory worker, quadriplegic from amyotrophic lateral sclerosis, who no

longer wants to linger in a hapless, dependent state, waiting and hoping for death.

A writer with extensive bony metastases from lung cancer, whose condition did not respond to chemotherapy or radiation, and who cannot accept the daily choice he must make between sedation and pain.[2]

These patients all meet the first criterion for justifiable euthanasia because their quality of life has become so intolerably low that they would prefer death to continued suffering.

A dying patient's quality of life can be diminished in a variety of ways. Many experience incredible amounts of physical pain in their last days, and they may find the side effects of pain medication unbearable. In addition to physical pain, some patients experience extreme emotional anguish after a debilitating illness or injury and may wish to be remembered only as the strong, independent person they were before their affliction. Still others dread the slow loss of control over mind

It WOULD Be cRUeL to PROLONG tHe iNeVitaBLe.

It'S iNeVitaBLe to PROLONG tHe cRUeLty.

and body that some diseases cause. In these rare circumstances, euthanasia may be the only way to relieve the suffering—whether physical or emotional—that these patients are enduring.

The Dying Patient's Choice

The second criterion for euthanasia to be ethical is that the patient must have no hope of recovery. "I believe that any assisted death should always be seen as a last option, as an extraordinary act that should be engaged in only when your physical health and quality of life have descended to a point that makes further living intolerable,"[3] states psychiatrist Stephen Jamison. In fact, such patients often choose euthanasia specifically *because* they have nothing to look forward to but a few more days, weeks, or months of pointless suffering. "Dying can be slow and agonizing, and some people simply want to get it over with,"[4] writes Marcia Angell, executive editor of the *New England Journal of Medicine*.

Because it is impossible to know how much another person is suffering, only the dying patient can make such a serious decision. This is why the third and most important requirement for euthanasia to be justified is that the dying patient specifically request it. When right-to-die advocates speak about euthanasia, they always mean *voluntary* euthanasia. The entire right-to-die movement is based on the idea that a patient's wishes should be respected—after all, why should doctors, lawmakers, ethicists, or anyone else claim to know what is best for them?

Moralism vs. Compassion

"Death is a taboo subject in American culture. And, like most taboo subjects, we both deny and fear it,"[5] write Derek Humphry and attorney Mary Clement in their book *Freedom to Die*. People today live longer and healthier lives than ever before. Most tend to avoid discussions of death and dying and do not want to deal with the problems dying people face.

Worse still, terminally ill patients' pleas for assistance in dying are ignored because of society's moralizing about the sanctity of life.

Opponents of euthanasia typically condemn it on the grounds that it violates the sanctity of life. To them, euthanasia is unethical because all human life is sacred. This is a noble sentiment, but it ignores the reality that a person's suffering can be so great that life is not worth living. Ethical arguments that "all human life should be preserved" provide little comfort to patients in extreme agony who want nothing more than the peace that only death can bring. As Angell puts it, "Moralism is no substitute for compassion."[6]

Nor should dying patients be denied a dignified, humane death because of the religious belief that all killing is wrong. Many Americans are atheists or agnostics, but even religious people often agree that euthanasia is ethical in certain circumstances. Episcopalian bishop John Shelby Spong argues that Christians must refine the traditional belief that all life is sacred: "The sacredness of my biological life is not ultimately found in my biological extension. It is found rather in the touch, the smile and the love of those to whom I can knowingly respond. When that ability to respond disappears permanently, so, I believe, does the meaning and value of my biological life."[7]

Spong gets to the heart of the issue: Euthanasia is not "killing" at all. Killing is the destruction of life. Many terminally ill patients feel that their life has already been destroyed by disease—euthanasia only hastens their already imminent death. The truth, uncomfortable as it is for many people, is that in rare instances euthanasia is the most compassionate way to relieve the suffering people face at the end of life. Euthanasia can be ethical, and dying patients should not be denied this simple, merciful option.

1. Derek Humphry, "Why I Believe in Voluntary Euthanasia," February 1995. www.islandnet. com/~deathnet/Humphry_essay.html.

2. Timothy E. Quill, *Death and Dignity: Making Choices and Taking Charge*. New York: W.W. Norton, 1993, pp. 156–57.

3. Stephen Jamison, *Final Acts of Love: Families, Friends, and Assisted Dying*. New York: G.P. Putnam's Sons, 1995, p. xix.

4. Marcia Angell, "No One Trusts the Dying," *Washington Post*, July 7, 1997, p. A19.

5. Derek Humphry and Mary Clement, *Freedom to Die: People, Politics, and the Right-to-Die Movement*. New York: St. Martin's, 1998, p. 21.

6. Quoted in Linda L. Emanual, ed., *Regulating How We Die: The Ethical, Medical, and Legal Issues Surrounding Physician-Assisted Suicide*. Cambridge, MA: Harvard University Press, 1998, p. 20.

7. John Shelby Spong, "In Defense of Assisted Suicide," *Human Quest*, May/June 1996, p. 11.

"Truly compassionate persons work to relieve suffering, not to eliminate the sufferer."

Euthanasia Is Unethical

Right-to-die activists contend that euthanasia is appropriate for terminally ill persons in great pain. Although many proponents of euthanasia are undoubtedly motivated by a desire to help dying patients, their logic is severely misguided. They propose that society should deal with its weakest, most vulnerable members—those who need the most care and attention— by killing them off. That is what euthanasia is: killing. Although right-to-die advocates prefer to use euphemisms such as "assisted death" and "death with dignity," these expressions cannot obscure the basic fact that euthanasia is the intentional killing of an innocent human being.

Why Is Killing Wrong?

Human life has innate value, and that is why the laws of every civilized society prohibit murder. Advocates of euthanasia deny that human beings have intrinsic worth: They argue that for patients who are in great pain, life has lost its value. But to accept these quality-of-life judgments is to accept the conclusion that some people have such a low quality of life that they do not deserve to live. This line of reasoning contradicts a fundamental purpose of law, which is to uphold the sanctity of life.

The world's major religions have all recognized the inherent immorality of killing. One of the Bible's ten commandments is "Thou shalt not kill." Life is a sacred gift from God, and only God may take it away. The Catholic Church has declared, "Only the Creator of life has the right to take away the life of the innocent."[1] Thus, the destruction of life is always wrong, even if it is done with the victim's consent, as in voluntary euthanasia, or even if the life destroyed is one's own, as in suicide. Even when done out of mercy, both acts are wrong because decisions about life and death are for God alone to make.

True Compassion

Right-to-die activists believe that killing can sometimes be merciful. Many of them sincerely believe that euthanasia is an act of compassion. Because of this, they rely on emotional pleas rather than reasoned arguments to defend euthanasia. Prominent right-to-die leader Timothy E. Quill advises his followers: *"Don't argue over positions."* Instead, he urges, tell stories "of the unrelieved suffering of dying patients."[2] Thus, proponents of euthanasia purposely try to argue around the fact that killing is wrong. As author Adam Wolfson puts it, "The American public is to be persuaded to accept assisted death not by arguments about right and wrong. . . . They are to be led to it via an unthinking compassion for those who suffer."[3]

"Unthinking compassion" is exactly what drives the right-to-die movement. As Pope John Paul II states, "Euthanasia must be called a *false* mercy, and indeed a disturbing 'perversion' of mercy,"[4] because truly compassionate persons can never condone killing. The phrase *mercy killing* is simply a contradiction in terms. As one opponent of euthanasia explains, "Compassion must, by definition, stop short of death. The Latin root of compassion actually means 'to suffer with.' If you kill the patient, there is no longer any 'with.' The patient has been abandoned."[5] Truly compassionate persons work to relieve suffering, not to eliminate the sufferer.

In addition to *mercy killing*, another misleading phrase is *death with dignity*. By stating that dying patients are entitled to death with dignity, right-to-die activists are implying that some deaths lack dignity. It is perfectly natural for people to fear old age and the dying process. But one fear that many people have—the fear that they will lose their dignity if they become weak or helpless at the end of life—is simply unfounded. All persons have a dignity, even as they lie dying. One writer explains basic human dignity as follows:

> The value of a human being . . . is intrinsic. Intrinsic value and dignity do not cease if you feel meaningless or suffer pain. It does not end if you are no longer young and attractive. . . . It is not based on your actions, productivity, or achievement. It is based on the fact that you are a person.[6]

Euthanasia is not necessary to achieve death with dignity, because no dying person's innate dignity is ever diminished by his or her suffering or weakness. And because all persons have intrinsic dignity, they deserve respect and care, not abandonment, as they near the end of life.

Choosing Life

Right-to-die activists often tell heartrending stories of people in great pain, for whom euthanasia was supposedly a great benefit. Yet for every one of these tales of desperation and heartbreak there are stories of courage and hope in which the tragedy of euthanasia was avoided. For example, Herbert Hendin, executive director of the American Suicide Foundation, tells the story of Tim, a young man who was diagnosed with acute myelocytic leukemia and given only a few months to live. At first Tim was fearful of the symptoms of his disease and the side effects of treatment, and he requested assisted suicide. However, says Hendin, after counseling, "his desperation subsided. He accepted medical treatment and used the remaining months of his life to become closer to his wife and parents. Two days before he died, Tim talked about what he would have missed without the opportunity for a loving parting."[7]

Euthanasia may sometimes seem justified; it is tempting to believe that it provides an easy solution to the tremendous suffering—and the fear of suffering—that people sometimes face at the end of life. But killing is never the right thing to do, and society must never condone, in the words of one author, "doctors who kill under the guidance of a deadly compassion and an abstract theory of dignity."[8] Instead, the best way to help dying patients is to improve the care and treatment they receive, so that at the end of life they can be sure that, like Tim, they will be surrounded by caring people who are committed to their well-being. The ethical choice is to respect the lives of all human beings, even as they confront death.

1. Quoted in John J. Paris, "Autonomy and Physician-Assisted Suicide," *America*, May 17, 1997, p. 13.

2. Quoted in Adam Wolfson, "Killing Off the Dying?" *Public Interest*, Spring 1998, p. 60.

3. Wolfson, "Killing Off the Dying?" p. 60.

4. John Paul II, *Evangelium Vitae* (*The Gospel of Life*), March 25, 1995, section 66. www.vatican.va/holy_father/john_paul_ii/encyclicals/john-paul-ii_encyclical_25-march-1995_evangelium-vitae_english.html.

5. Robin Bernhoft, "How We Can Win the Compassion Debate," *Citizen Magazine*, June 24, 1996. www.aapainmanage.org/aapm/art1.htm.

6. John F. Kavanaugh, "Death's Dignity," *America*, March 8, 1997, p.18.

7. Quoted in House Committee on the Judiciary, Subcommittee on the Constitution, *Oversight Hearing: Assisted Suicide in the United States*, 104th Cong., 2nd sess., 29 April 1996. www.house.gov/judiciary/2169.htm.

8. Wolfson, "Killing Off the Dying?" p. 70.

"There is no logical reason that active killing should be any more or less acceptable than so-called passive means of hastening death."

There Is No Difference Between Active and Passive Euthanasia

The term *euthanasia* is often used to mean different things. Traditional thinking on the subject distinguishes between "passive" euthanasia—in which life-sustaining treatment, such as an artificial respirator, is withdrawn—and "active" euthanasia—in which a doctor intentionally causes death by administering a lethal dose of medication. Passive euthanasia is legal in the United States and is widely accepted while active euthanasia is not. Philosopher Robert D. Lane sums up this reasoning: "It has long been held that the distinction between active and passive euthanasia is crucial for medical ethics. The idea is that although it may be permissible in some cases to withhold treatment and allow a patient to die, it is never permissible to take any direct action to bring about that death."[1]

An Arbitrary Distinction

This is the view endorsed by both the American Medical Association and the Catholic Church, and it is a distinction the Supreme Court has repeatedly upheld. In reality, however-er, there is no logical reason that active killing should be any more or less acceptable than so-called passive means of has-tening death.

The logic is deceptively simple: "Killing" is wrong, "letting die" is not. Yet examining the real-life situations in which euthanasia occurs reveals that the line between killing and let-ting die is easily blurred. For example, doctors are obliged to provide relief from pain even when the medication necessary to control extreme pain may shorten the life of the patient. If death occurs in such a situation, who can tell whether the doc-tor has merely treated the patient or has killed him? There are more shades of gray surrounding euthanasia than many peo-ple want to admit.

The most passive form of euthanasia is the discontinuation of artificial life-support systems for a patient in an irreversible coma. The classic example of this is the 1976 case of the comatose patient Karen Ann Quinlan and her parents' request that she be removed from her artificial respirator. The New Jersey Supreme Court finally ruled that Quinlan's parents, acting on her behalf, could remove the respirator. This estab-lished a patient's legal right to refuse unwanted medical treat-ment, even if to do so would result in the patient's death.

Causing Death

The right to refuse treatment benefits patients. But it should be viewed as just one of the options patients have for retain-ing control over their deaths. Opponents of euthanasia like to think that patients refuse treatment only when it is invasive or inappropriate, not because they want to die. But as one doc-tor explains, in real-life situations, "when a dying patient's life supports are turned off, it is seldom because the treatment itself is burdensome, but mainly because the patient or family wants to hasten death."[2]

Since shutting off life supports causes death just as surely as a more active form of euthanasia would, then it follows that if a suffering patient requests it, giving that patient a lethal injection should be just as permissible as terminating his or her treatment. As right-to-die activist Barbara Dority explains, "Both remain equivalent morally. Motivated by the same compassion, they both initiate active steps that will lead to the patient's death."[3]

Furthermore, discontinuing life support is not passive at all. Turning off a machine or disconnecting a respirator is an action, one that would be considered murder if it occurred against a patient's will. What makes the act morally permissible is not whether the patient dies of natural causes or as a result of the doctor's action, but because the patient requests it (or, in the case of comatose patients, because family members request it on their behalf). Thus, it is respect for the wishes of the patient and the desire to end his or her suffering that makes euthanasia justifiable, not whether the act itself is passive or active.

The absurdity of trying to limit euthanasia to the termination of treatment was revealed in the 1990 court case of Nancy Cruzan. After a severe car crash in 1983, Cruzan, like Quinlan, was left brain dead and comatose, able to live only with the help of a machine. As in the Quinlan case, Cruzan's parents wanted this machine removed. However, the machine consisted of intravenous feeding tubes that provided Cruzan with hydration and nutrition. The Missouri Supreme Court felt that to remove the feeding tubes would be to intentionally and actively kill Cruzan through starvation. Although the U.S. Supreme Court ruled that, under Missouri law, Cruzan's parents could not act on her behalf, it also stated that the tubes constituted a form of treatment that Cruzan could refuse if she were competent. In *Cruzan v. Missouri Department of Health*, Justice Sandra Day O'Connor wrote in her concurring opinion, "I agree that a protected liberty interest in refusing unwanted medical treatment may be inferred from our prior decisions, . . . and that the refusal of artificially delivered food and water is encompassed within that liberty interest."[4]

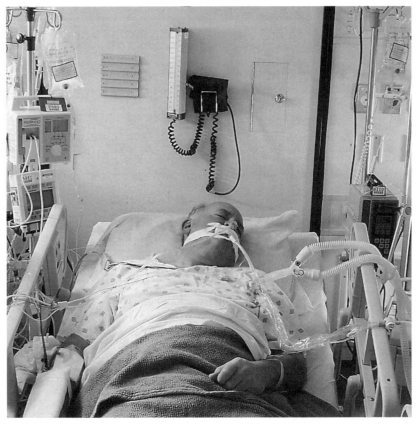

Modern medicine has made it possible to keep a person who is in a "persistent vegetative state" alive once his or her mind has ceased to function, but it is often expensive and emotionally stressful for the patient's family. Individuals may sign advance directives for living wills indicating whether or not they want their lives prolonged in this manner, or family members may sometimes request passive euthanasia on the patient's behalf.

A More Humane Option

A few months after the trial, Missouri's attorney general changed his mind and decided to allow Cruzan's parents to end their daughter's suffering. The feeding tubes were removed, and Cruzan died twelve days later. Obviously, Cruzan was starved to death. Only because of the irrelevant distinction between killing and letting die were Cruzan's parents forced to maintain the inane premise that they were merely terminating treatment. Moreover, once the decision to terminate her treatment was made, there was no reason why her death should not have been hastened in a more humane manner.

In another Supreme Court case, this time over physician-assisted suicide, six eminent philosophers submitted a brief to the Court in which they argued: "From a patient's point of view, there is no morally pertinent difference between a doctor's terminating treatment that keeps him alive, if that is what he wishes, and a doctor's helping him to end his own life by providing lethal pills he may take himself . . . except that the latter may be quicker and more humane."[5] Physician-assisted death, an active form of euthanasia, is actually preferable to letting a patient die because doctors have access to medications that can end life quickly and painlessly. Death by starvation, on the other hand, is a long, harrowing ordeal. Patients should not be forced to undergo a slow, painful death just because society has labeled it a form of passive euthanasia.

Discriminating Against the Terminally Ill

In fact, laws that allow only passive and not active euthanasia violate the rights of many terminally ill patients. Some terminally ill patients are allowed to hasten their deaths through the refusal of treatment, but others, who may be suffering just as much but are not dependent on machines, are denied the means to control their deaths.

This discrimination prolongs the suffering of some but not others. As one doctor explains, "Merely having the right to refuse life-sustaining treatment does not solve the problem of prolonged dying for all patients."[6] She advocates physician-assisted suicide (PAS), in which a doctor provides lethal pills and the patient decides when to take them. But as Derek Humphry and Mary Clement point out, "PAS is fine as far as it goes, enabling those patients who can ingest huge overdoses to have a happy release. But it excludes those patients who . . . have had surgery to remove the swallowing and digestive organs, or those who cannot keep down liquids and solids."[7] Ethicist Nicholas Dixon argues, "Fairness requires that if we legalize physician-assisted suicide, then we also make active euthanasia legally available to patients who are physically unable to commit physician-assisted suicide or who prefer to die by lethal injections."[8] Although it shocks some people, physician-administered lethal injection is a quick, painless means of ending a patient's life. There is no reason why patients should be denied this humane option, other than the stigma attached to lethal injections as an active form of euthanasia.

All forms of voluntary euthanasia—including the withdrawal of treatment, doctor-prescribed suicide pills, and physician-administered lethal injection—are morally equivalent because they all result in the death of the patient. However, some means of hastening death are more humane than others, and dying patients should not be limited only to those that society feels are passive. Doctors and lawmakers should concern themselves with what the patient wants rather than quibbling over whether a given action constitutes "killing" or "letting die." In the end, the distinction only really serves to portray euthanasia as a black-and-white issue and to obscure the fact that active killing is often the most compassionate, justifiable option for persons who sincerely want to die.

1. Robert D. Lane and Richard Dunstan, "Euthanasia: The Debate Continues," Institute of Practical Philosophy, August 1995. www.mala.bc.ca/www/ipp/euthanas.htm.

2. Marcia Angell, "No One Trusts the Dying," *Washington Post*, July 7, 1997, p. A19.

3. Barbara Dority, "The Ultimate Liberty," *Humanist*, July/August 1997, p. 16.

4. *Cruzan v. Missouri Department of Health*, opinion text. www.soros.org/debate/cruzan.htm.

5. Ronald Dworkin et al., "Assisted Suicide: The Philosophers' Brief," *New York Review of Books*, March 27, 1997, p. 35.

6. Quoted in Linda L. Emanual, ed., *Regulating How We Die: The Ethical, Medical, and Legal Issues Surrounding Physician-Assisted Suicide.* Cambridge, MA: Harvard University Press, 1998, p. 20.

7. Derek Humphry and Mary Clement, *Freedom to Die: People, Politics, and the Right-to-Die Movement.* New York, St. Martin's, 1998, p. 336.

8. Nicholas Dixon, "On the Difference Between Physician-Assisted Suicide and Active Euthanasia," *Hastings Center Report*, September/October 1998, p. 29.

"In passive euthanasia, life-prolonging treatment is withdrawn and a terminal illness is allowed to run its natural course. The underlying illness, not the doctor or anyone else, causes death."

There Is a Difference Between Active and Passive Euthanasia

A false claim made by many right-to-die activists is that all forms of euthanasia are the same. According to their logic, since it is morally acceptable to disconnect the life-support system of a brain-dead, comatose patient, then it should also be acceptable to administer a lethal injection to any patient who requests one. But these two forms of euthanasia are not the same at all; that is why religious leaders, the medical establishment, and the U.S. legal system have all recognized the difference between passive euthanasia, in which treatment is withdrawn and patients are allowed to die, and the active killing of patients with lethal medications.

In passive euthanasia, life-prolonging treatment is withdrawn and a terminal illness is allowed to run its natural course. The underlying illness, not the doctor or anyone else, causes death. Passive euthanasia occurs when a patient or family members feel that medical interventions to prolong life are unbearably painful, invasive, or otherwise inappropriate. Patients have the right to reject any procedure or medication that they feel is simply not worth it.

The Legal Necessity of Passive Euthanasia

This right to reject medical treatments is essential to individual liberty. To understand why, just imagine what a hospital stay would be like if a patient was forced to accept any treatment doctors recommended. As the New York State Task Force on Life and the Law writes, "A prohibition on the refusal of treatment would . . . require the widespread restraint of patients unwilling to submit to invasive procedures at the end of their lives. Such a policy would be an abuse of medicine, placing patients at the mercy of every technological advance."[1]

Because the right to refuse treatment is essential to avoid this horrific scenario, the courts have ruled that this right should not be limited in any way. This means that even if it will result in death, patients may still refuse treatment. By withdrawing life supports, the doctor is only respecting the patient's wishes regarding medical treatment, not intending the death of the patient. That the patient may be refusing treatment because he wants to die is irrelevant—the right itself is a safeguard to prevent doctors from abusing their power, not an acceptance that hastening death is ever appropriate.

The Moral Distinction Between Active and Passive Euthanasia

Yet the right to refuse treatment is not just a legal necessity: The idea that patients should be allowed to die a natural death has a strong moral basis as well. In its 1980 *Declaration on Euthanasia*, the Catholic Church emphatically stated that "nothing and no one can in any way permit the killing of an innocent human being," even "one suffering from an incurable disease, or a person who is dying."[2] Yet the church acknowledged that "when inevitable death is imminent" it is permissible "to refuse forms of treatment that would only secure a precarious and burdensome prolongation of life."[3]

Active euthanasia, on the other hand, is often termed *mercy killing* precisely because it involves the intentional killing of a patient. Even if the killing is medicalized and done with pills or a lethal injection, it is still killing. Active euthanasia is performed to put a person out of his misery in much the same way one would shoot a wounded horse or put a family pet to sleep. Mercy killing, when applied to human beings, is an abhorrent, immoral practice that religious authorities and the American Medical Association rightly condemn.

Confusion in the Courts

It is obvious that killing and letting die are not at all the same. Yet right-to-die activists sought to deny this simple truth in a recent court case over physician-assisted suicide, *Washington v. Glucksberg*. Worse, one of the highest courts in the nation succumbed to their legal sophistry. In March 1996 the Ninth Circuit Court of Appeals ruled that there was "no ethical or constitutionally cognizable difference between a doctor's pulling the plug on a respirator and his prescribing drugs which will permit a terminally ill patient to end his own life," because "the death of the patient is the intended result in one case as surely as in the other."[4]

The judges of the Ninth Circuit were simply wrong to claim that whenever futile or unwanted treatments are withdrawn the death of the patient is the ultimate goal. Professor George Annas explains why the judges' reasoning is unsound: "Since the vast majority of deaths in hospitals occur after some medical intervention is refused or deemed useless, under the court's logic there is an epidemic of suicide and homicide in the nations' hospitals—a patently absurd conclusion."[5]

The case of Karen Ann Quinlan clearly shows that doctors do not intend death when they discontinue treatment. Karen Ann Quinlan was a young woman who had collapsed into an irreversible coma. Her parents felt that the artificial respirator that was helping her breathe was invasive. However, even after the respirator was removed, Quinlan lived for another nine years for two reasons: 1) Quinlan's doctors slowly weaned her lungs off the respirator over the course of weeks so that she would have the best chance of being able to breathe on her own, and 2) Quinlan's parents did not want her intravenous feeding tubes removed. Clearly, although they discontinued Quinlan's treatment knowing that she *might* die, neither her parents nor her doctors wanted to end her life.

Intent Is the Key

It is not difficult to see where the judges of the Ninth Circuit erred. In some sense, doctors do cause the death of some patients when they disconnect life-support systems. However, as previously discussed, doctors do so out of respect for the right to refuse treatment, not to hasten the death of the patient. Many types of medical intervention—for example, an unsuccessful surgical procedure—may result in the death of a patient, but it does not follow that the purpose of the procedure was to end the life of the patient.

Intent is the key in these seemingly ambiguous cases. An excellent example of this is the doctrine of double effect. Physicians have a duty to provide adequate medication to relieve pain, yet high doses of pain relievers such as morphine can be lethal. The doctrine of double effect, a respected principle of medical ethics, holds that a doctor may prescribe high doses of morphine in order to relieve pain. If the dose also results in the death of the patient (the double effect), the doctor's act is considered ethical as long as his intent was only to relieve pain. For similar reasons, intending to remove unduly burdensome treatment is acceptable even if, as a secondary effect, it ends up causing death.

Killing and Letting Die Are Not the Same

Fortunately for the nation, in 1997 the Supreme Court unanimously overturned the ruling of the Ninth Circuit and upheld the distinction between passive euthanasia and physician-assisted suicide. "When a patient refuses life-saving treatment, he dies from an underlying fatal disease or pathology," writes Chief Justice William Rehnquist, "but if a patient ingests lethal medication prescribed by a physician, he is killed by that medication." He added that, in prior rulings, the Court "certainly gave no intimation that the right to refuse unwanted medical treatment could be somehow transmuted into a right to assistance in committing suicide." The right to refuse treatment is deeply imbedded in an individual's right to privacy, Rehnquist explained, but the right to be killed "has never enjoyed similar legal protection. Indeed, the two acts are widely and reasonably regarded as quite distinct."[6]

Right-to-die activists often lump all forms of euthanasia together in an attempt to confuse the issues. However, there are important ethical differences between active and passive euthanasia. Killing and allowing to die are not the same.

1. New York State Task Force on Life and the Law, *When Death Is Sought: Assisted Suicide and Euthanasia in the Medical Context.* New York State Department of Health, May 1994, p. 75. www.health.state.ny.us/nysdoh/provider/death.htm.

2. Sacred Congregation for the Doctrine of the Faith, "Declaration on Euthanasia," May 5, 1980. http://listserv.american.edu/catholic/church/vatican/cdfeuth.txt.

3. Sacred Congregation for the Doctrine of the Faith, "Declaration on Euthanasia."

4. Quoted in Yale Kamisar, "The Reasons So Many People Support Physician-Assisted Suicide—and Why These Reasons Are Not Convincing," *Issues in Law & Medicine*, Fall 1996, p. 120.

5. Quoted in Kamisar, "The Reasons So Many People Support Physician-Assisted Suicide," p. 126.

6. *Washington v. Glucksberg*, opinion text. http://supct.law.cornell.edu/supct/html/96-110.ZO.html.

CHAPTER 2

Should
Physicians
Participate in
Euthanasia?

"Physician-assisted suicide is unethical and fundamentally inconsistent with the pledge physicians make to devote themselves to healing and to life."

Physician-Assisted Suicide Violates Medical Ethics

The euthanasia debate is of particular importance to physicians. As Faye J. Girsh of the Hemlock Society explains, if a person wants to die "quickly, safely, peacefully and non-violently" then "it is necessary for physicians to be the agents of death . . . since the best means to accomplish this is medication that only doctors can prescribe."[1] Thus, physicians must ask themselves: Should members of the healing profession also become "agents of death"?

The Importance of Medical Ethics

The simple answer to this question can be found in the Hippocratic oath, the pledge that doctors make never to harm their patients. Although it dates back to ancient Greece, it nevertheless "articulates a coherent, rational, and indeed wise, vision of the art of medicine."[2] Ancient Greek physicians formulated the Hippocratic oath because they recognized that physicians hold a great deal of power over their patients. "The same medications that alleviate suffering can cause horrible side effects,"[3] writes one doctor. Patients who submit to even the most basic surgical procedures are literally putting their lives in doctors' hands. The doctor-patient relationship is truly a sacred trust—one that would quickly disintegrate if doctors were allowed to kill their patients.

To ensure that doctors do not abuse their power, the medical profession has set voluntary limits on itself. These limits take the form of medical ethics. The Hippocratic oath is the original statement of medical ethics, and many medical school graduates still take it today. Doctors who take the oath pledge never to take advantage of their patients' weakness. They promise to refrain from having sex with their patients, for example. They also pledge, "I will neither give a deadly drug to anybody if asked for it, nor will I make a suggestion to this effect."[4] Thus, the Hippocratic oath, a document that has served as the ethical cornerstone of the medical profession for centuries, clearly condemns physician-assisted suicide and euthanasia.

Obviously, as medical science has become more complex over the centuries, so have the ethical principles to which doctors must adhere. Medical societies have developed new and more specific guidelines to protect patients. But the first of these guidelines has always been that physicians must never intentionally harm their patients, either by giving them the means to commit suicide or by killing them outright. The American Medical Association states, "Physician-assisted suicide is unethical and fundamentally inconsistent with the pledge physicians make to devote themselves to healing and to life."[5]

Acknowledging That Death Is Inevitable

This does not mean that doctors have an absolute duty to prolong life. Doctors should not always see death as the enemy but instead allow nature to take its course when a patient has been overmastered by disease:

> When we decide with a patient or family that the time has come to withdraw life-support measures

and allow a patient to die, it represents a humble recognition of the limits of medicine and a submission to forces beyond our control. By contrast, in administering a lethal injection, even to a consenting patient, we seem to overstep our bounds, as though wresting from nature something that is not properly ours.[6]

In addition, doctors sometimes unintentionally cause the death of their patients. This can happen in a variety of ways. For example, a patient may choose to undergo a risky, experimental procedure that ends up killing him or her. Or, in trying to control a patient's pain, doctors might prescribe doses of medication that are so high that they have a chance of killing the patient. But in these situations, the doctors are trying to help their patients, not kill them.

Patient Autonomy Has Limits

Some patients feel that the only way a doctor can help them is to provide them with the means to commit suicide. One principle of medical ethics, that of patient autonomy, holds that doctors should respect the wishes of their patients. But this principle is far from absolute; doctors are certainly under no obligation to do whatever their patient asks of them. For example, a doctor would not provide steroids to an athlete just because he requests them because doing so would not be in the patient's best interests. Likewise, doctors have a duty to refuse requests for physician-assisted suicide. As physician Leon R. Kass explains, "In forswearing the giving of poison *if asked for it*, the Hippocratic physician rejects the view that the patient's choice for death can make killing him—or assisting his suicide—right."[7]

Playing God

Thus, doctors may only accede to patient requests when doing so will benefit the patient. Proponents, however, reply that euthanasia does help the patient because it relieves suffering. According to them, doctors should be permitted to assist in suicide when they agree that it is in the patient's best interests. The problem with this scenario is that doctors should never make such judgments.

How might a doctor go about deciding whether a patient would benefit from being killed? First, he would have to be sure that the patient has no hope for recovery. This is difficult enough. Next, he would have to be confident that the patient was using sound judgment and was not simply confused or depressed from the effects of illness or medication. This is almost impossible, which is why, in the words of one physician, "The law has traditionally erred on the side of regarding attempted suicide as an intrinsically irrational decision, constituting *prima facie* [self-evident] evidence of psychiatric incompetence."[8]

Finally, and most disturbingly, the doctor would have to discern how much pain the patient was experiencing. What amount of pain is necessary to justify euthanasia? How could a doctor possibly decide that, yes, this patient here should be

helped to die, but no, that patient there is not suffering enough and his request for suicide should be refused? There is no quality-of-life measuring stick; such assessments are entirely subjective. Doctors *cannot* and *must not* decide whether death would benefit a given patient because such decisions would be tantamount to playing God.

Professional Integrity

Still, euthanasia supporters will say, there are cases in which a patient sincerely wants to die and a doctor firmly believes the request should be granted. But even in these cases, doctors should not assist in suicide because it would violate their professional integrity. There are some things doctors must never do simply because they are doctors. For example, doctors do not participate in capital punishment—even though some doctors support the death penalty, and even though physician participation in executions might make them quicker and more humane. No matter what their individual beliefs about the death penalty are, doctors do not participate in executions because it would violate the physician's role as a healer. "A person can choose to be a physician, but he cannot simply choose what physicianship means,"[9] says Kass.

Likewise, it is contrary to the goals of medicine for doctors to become agents of death. "For more than two millennia," writes Kass, "the reigning medical ethic, mindful that the power to cure is also the power to kill, has held an inviolable rule, 'Doctors must not kill.'"[10] There is no reason why doctors should now violate this ancient taboo. No matter how complex the ethics of medical practice become, doctors must always adhere to one simple maxim: "First, do no harm."

1. Faye J. Girsh, "The Case for Physician Aid in Dying," *Journal of the Hippocratic Society*, Fall 1997, p. 9.

2. Leon R. Kass and Nelson Lund, "Courting Death: Assisted Suicide, Doctors, and the Law," *Commentary*, December 1996, p. 20.

3. Louis Vernacchio, "Physician-Assisted Suicide: Reflections of a Young Doctor," *America*, August 31, 1996, p. 14.

4. Quoted in Kass and Lund, "Courting Death," p. 19.

5. Quoted in House Committee on the Judiciary, Subcommittee on the Constitution, *Oversight Hearing: Assisted Suicide in the United States*, 104th Cong., 2nd sess., April 29, 1996. www.house.gov/judiciary/2170.htm.

6. Thomas J. Gates, "Euthanasia and Assisted Suicide: A Family Practice Perspective," *American Family Physician*, May 15, 1997. www.aafp.org/afp/970515ap/society.html.

7. Quoted in Michael M. Uhlmann, ed., *Last Rights?: Assisted Suicide and Euthanasia Debated*. Grand Rapids, MI: William B. Eerdmans, 1998, p. 301.

8. Quoted in Uhlmann, *Last Rights?*, p. 354.

9. Quoted in Uhlmann, *Last Rights?*, p. 301.

10. Quoted in Uhlmann, *Last Rights?*, p. 297.

"One of medicine's highest missions is to allow hopelessly ill persons to die with as much comfort, control, and dignity as possible."

Physician-Assisted Suicide Does Not Violate Medical Ethics

Doctors must always act in the best interests of their patients. However, in many situations, it can be difficult for a doctor to determine the right thing to do. When moral dilemmas arise—as they often do when doctors are forced to make life-or-death decisions—medical ethics help physicians determine the proper course of action. Euthanasia is such a moral dilemma. Although it violates society's taboo against killing, physician-assisted suicide is actually consistent with medical ethics if a hopelessly ill person requests it and the doctor agrees that the request is rational.

The Hippocratic Oath

Much of the opposition to physician-assisted suicide is based on the fact that the Hippocratic oath forbids it. Having originated with the ancient Greeks somewhere between the sixth and first century B.C., the Hippocratic oath is the first known effort by physicians to define rules that should govern the practice of medicine. Because of its venerable roots, the oath is still highly regarded by many doctors today.

Contrary to popular belief, however, few physicians have actually taken the oath. "Many physicians have never even read it, much less sworn to it," write Derek Humphry and Mary Clement. "Few medical schools require its reading at graduation ceremonies."[1] This is because the medical establishment has recognized that, while the overall ideals set forth in the Hippocratic oath remain valuable, many of its specifics, such as its prohibition of abortion, have become obsolete. In the two millennia since the oath was first formulated, medical technology has far surpassed what was available to the ancient Greeks, and the ethical dilemmas faced by physicians have consequently changed. "Realistically," states one author, "the Hippocratic oath should be viewed as a quaint and admirable relic of the distant past, part of the truly glorious history of medicine—but not as a restriction on physicians who want to provide their patients with the best possible care."[2]

"First, Do No Harm"

The Hippocratic oath's prohibition on euthanasia and physician-assisted suicide is part of its more general message of *"Primum non nocere,"* or "First, do no harm." (Although it does not appear in the Hippocratic oath, this maxim is, like the oath, attributed to the ancient Greek physician Hippocrates.) "First, do no harm" is a vital principle of medical ethics, but it is not as simple as it sounds. The reality is that doctors sometimes do harm patients. For example, chemotherapy, which can save a cancer patient's life, is painful, debilitating, and actually kills the patient's cells. Many other modern medical treatments can be seen as both a benefit and a harm. In these situations it is up to the patient, not the doctor, to determine whether a given treatment is harmful or beneficial.

The Hippocratic oath's prohibition on assisted suicide is a good general rule for doctors to follow since death usually does constitute a great harm. But when death will cause less harm than prolonged suffering, the guideline of "First, do no harm" does not apply. Only the patient can decide when this is the case. The ancient Greeks could not know that medical science would one day enable people to live so long that many patients would see euthanasia as a benefit, but the right-to-die movement is evidence that many people do, and their wishes must prevail over the archaic guideline found in the Hippocratic oath.

Caring Beyond Curing

Much of the opposition to physician-assisted dying is due to a widespread lack of understanding of what a doctor's duties actually are. The goal of medicine is not, as many people assume, simply to heal or to preserve life. Instead, writes Marcia Angell, executive editor of the *New England Journal of Medicine*, "The highest ethical imperative of doctors should be to provide care in whatever way best serves patients' interests, in accord with each patient's wishes, not with a theoretical commitment to preserve life no matter what the cost in suffering."[3] Doctors actually have two responsibilities to patients, as physician Timothy E. Quill explains: "One is to preserve life and the other is to relieve human suffering. Usually you are trying to do both, . . . but in end-of-life care you take relief of suffering as your priority."[4]

Thus, a doctor's responsibility to care for his or her patient does not end when all hope for a cure is gone. When death is imminent, doctors still have a duty to respect patients' wishes and to do everything possible to relieve suffering and help their patients achieve a good death. "One of medicine's highest missions is to allow hopelessly ill persons to die with as much comfort, control, and dignity as possible,"[5] says Quill.

The Doctor-Patient Relationship

Aware of their duty to relieve end-of-life suffering, many physicians currently hasten the deaths of their patients through a variety of methods. They may, at the patient's request, withdraw lifesaving treatment—this may mean the removal of a respirator or a feeding tube, or, less obviously, a doctor might not treat an infection with antibiotics, thus allowing an elderly patient to develop pneumonia or some other illness. Doctors also covertly hasten death through the use of pain-control medications such as morphine. Or the doctor may, illegally, provide the patient with the means to commit suicide, for example, by leaving a large bottle of sleeping pills on the patient's bedside table.

The problem with these methods is that they occur in secret. "These are doctors who want desperately to serve the best interests of their patients," writes one right-to-die activist. "Nevertheless, there are dangers in the kind of situation we have today, in which good doctors must break the law to help their patients, with no safeguards or guidelines. That is why the laws need to be changed."[6] Openly acknowledging that physician-assisted dying is sometimes justified would reduce the potential for abuse. It would also enhance the trust that people have in doctors because it would mean that patients could count on doctors to respect their wishes regarding assisted suicide. In contrast, "the relationship can only erode further when a patient cannot be certain that the physician will follow his or her wishes."[7]

The Role of Physicians

Some opponents of physician-assisted dying admit that requests for physician-assisted suicide are valid but insist that doctors should not be the ones to grant them because it might tarnish their image as healers. But, again, doctors are not simply healers working to preserve life, they must also be caregivers working to relieve suffering. And the practical realities of dying make it crucial that physicians participate in the process because only physicians have access to the knowledge and medicines necessary to ensure a swift and humane death.

Many dying patients want assistance in suicide. When the patient is suffering, has no hope for recovery, and when the

request to die is rational and uncoerced, then a doctor's dual obligation to relieve suffering and to respect patients' wishes dictate that such requests be granted. In addition, the doctor's duty not to harm is not violated if death would cause less harm to the patient than prolonging unnecessary suffering. In these circumstances, doctors have a medical duty to grant requests for assisted suicide.

1. Derek Humphry and Mary Clement, *Freedom to Die: People, Politics, and the Right-to-Die Movement.* New York: St. Martin's, 1998, p. 198.

2. William H.A. Carr, "Updating the Physician's Oath," *Saturday Evening Post,* September/ October 1995, p. 51.

3. Marcia Angell, "The Supreme Court and Physician-Assisted Suicide—the Ultimate Right," *New England Journal of Medicine*, January 2, 1997, p. 52.

4. Timothy E. Quill, "In the Name of Mercy," *People Weekly*, April 7, 1997, p. 137.

5. Timothy E. Quill, *Death and Dignity: Making Choices and Taking Charge*. New York: W.W. Norton, 1993, p. 156.

6. Carr, "Updating the Physician's Oath," p. 70.

7. Death with Dignity Education Center fact sheet, "Misconceptions in the Debate on Death with Dignity," January 1997.

CHAPTER 3

Should Voluntary Euthanasia Be Legalized?

"The right to life, liberty, and the pursuit of happiness includes the right to die with dignity."

Individuals Have a Right to Die

A central tenet of individual liberty is that individuals have the right to do as they wish with their own bodies so long as it does not harm others. Choosing how to die is the last decision a person makes, and many people feel it is a crucial part of their freedom to live their lives as they see fit. "Individuals in a free world must be able to decide this ultimate question about their lives,"[1] says the Hemlock Society's executive director, Faye J. Girsh.

The Ultimate Human Right

Allowing people to die in the manner of their choosing is consistent with the American concepts of individual liberty and limited government, as envisioned by the founding fathers. "The right to life, liberty, and the pursuit of happiness includes the right to die with dignity," says Libertarian Party chairman Steve Dasbach. "The power to decide how and when to die should reside solely with the individual patient, not with doctors, family members—and especially not with the government."[2]

The government has no business crafting laws that dictate how people can and cannot die. As federal appeals court judge Roger J. Miner asks, "What interest can the state possibly have in requiring the prolongation of a life that is all but ended? And what business is it of the state to require the continuation of agony when the result is imminent and inevitable?"[3] When the government restricts a person's very personal end-of-life decisions, it performs a great injustice. As law professor Ronald Dworkin writes, "Making someone die in a way that others approve, but that he believes contradicts his own dignity, is a serious, unjustified, unnecessary form of tyranny."[4]

Laws against euthanasia are not only unjust because they violate individual privacy, but they are also malicious and unconscionable because they prolong a person's suffering against his or her will. "It is inhumane, cruel and even barbaric to make a suffering person, whose death is inevitable, live longer than he or she wishes,"[5] writes Girsh. Activist Barbara Dority explains, "We in the right-to-die movement are determined to put an end to the anguish being unjustly inflicted upon the dying and their loved ones. The obscenity of the state denying its citizens the ultimate human and civil right to control their own lives and bodies is intolerable."[6]

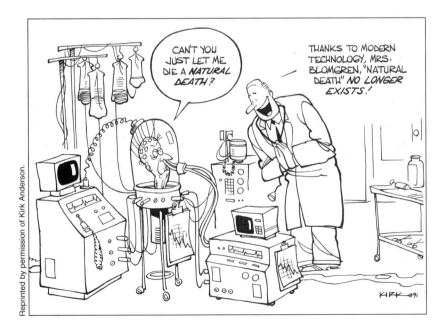

Understanding the Right-to-Die Movement

Some people support euthanasia in certain circumstances but are uncomfortable with the idea that the United States should formally give its citizens a legal right to end their lives. Two points are needed to clarify the widespread confusion about what the phrase *right to die* means, and why such a right is so important. First, the right to die should be a very limited right: Euthanasia is not an option that should be given to the depressed or mentally ill or to children, and it is not an option to be forced on anyone who objects to the act. The right to die is more properly described as "the right of mentally competent, terminally ill individuals to choose a death with dignity and without needless suffering."[7]

Second, it is necessary that the federal government recognize a constitutionally protected right to euthanasia because without such federal protection, state legislatures will deprive citizens of this freedom. This is the current legal status of euthanasia in America: The Constitution does not address the issue, so the states are allowed to ban or to permit euthanasia and physician-assisted suicide as they see fit.

In fact, just because the Constitution does not specifically address euthanasia does not mean that individuals do not have a right to die. The Ninth Amendment in the Bill of Rights states, "The enumeration in the Constitution of certain rights shall not be construed to deny or disparage others retained by the people." The right to die is one of these unenumerated rights protected by the Ninth Amendment. The Libertarian Party's Dasbach explains that it "is a basic human right that predates the Constitution and is protected by it. It can be neither granted nor taken away by politicians and judges."[8]

Still, over thirty-five states expressly forbid physician-assisted dying. Only Oregon has passed a law that respects the right of a terminally ill patient to control the timing and manner of his or her death, and that law was passed only after years of expensive court battles and two referenda in which Oregon voters expressed their support for the law. Oregon is clearly an exceptional case, and the victory of the right-to-die movement there will be hard to duplicate. In most of the country, religious groups are able to use their considerable resources to block assisted suicide legislation. Unless dying patients have a constitutionally protected right to die, their ability to achieve a humane death will be taken away by voters who want to impose their religious beliefs on others.

Separation of Church and State

Laws against murder can be justified on the grounds that murder causes harm to the victim. However, laws against euthanasia and assisted suicide cannot be similarly grounded because in such cases an individual has determined that death with dignity would be a benefit rather than a harm. Instead, these laws are based on the religious belief that all human life must be preserved.

Many people believe that life is sacred and that it should be preserved at all costs. Such individuals are entitled to their opinions, but these opinions are not a valid basis for making voluntary euthanasia or assisted suicide a crime. As federal appeals court judge Stephen Reinhardt writes:

> Those who believe strongly that death must come without physician assistance are free to follow that creed, be they doctors or patients. They are not free, however, to force their views, their religious convictions, or their philosophies on all other members of a democratic society, and compel those whose values differ with theirs to die painful, protracted, and agonizing deaths.[9]

Professor Dworkin explains, "The Constitution does not allow states to justify policy on grounds of religious doctrine."[10]

Modern Medicine Confronts an Ancient Dilemma

The modern right-to-die movement has been a source of major controversy only since the 1980s, but the debate over mercy killing is not a new one. Some people have always died badly, and some people have always been unable to deal with the reality that a person might prefer death to a life filled with suffering. But today the debate over euthanasia is more urgent than ever.

More people are dying painful, lingering deaths than ever before. Doctors today have an incredible ability to prolong life, but as average life expectancy has increased, so has the time it takes the average person to die. For example, at the beginning of the twentieth century most Americans died at home, and quickly, from illnesses such as pneumonia or influenza. Today over 80 percent of Americans die in the hospital, and they are more likely to die from conditions such as cancer, heart disease, or Lou Gehrig's disease—conditions that can lead to a slow, agonizing death. While modern medicine has made people's lives better, it has made their deaths worse.

"Both the boundaries and the quality of life have been extended beyond anything our ancestors could have imagined," testified Episcopalian bishop John Shelby Spong before a congressional committee on physician-assisted suicide. This changing medical environment makes it more important than ever that the right to die with dignity be recognized. "We live in a country that endows its citizens with certain inalienable rights," he concluded. "Among those rights, newly given, as a peculiar gift of this modern world, is the right to participate in the management of our own deaths."[11] It is wrong for the government to deny its citizens this simple, basic human right.

1. Faye J. Girsh, "The Case for Physician Aid in Dying," *Journal of the Hippocratic Society*, Fall 1997, p. 10.

2. Quoted in Libertarian Party press release, January 9, 1997. www.lp.org/rel/970109-suicide.html.

3. Quoted in Barbara Dority, "'In the Hands of the People': Recent Victories of the Death-with-Dignity Movement," *Humanist*, July/August 1996, p. 7.

4. Quoted in Michael M. Uhlmann, ed., *Last Rights?: Assisted Suicide and Euthanasia Debated.* Grand Rapids, MI: William B. Eerdmans, 1998, p. 93.

5. Girsh, "The Case for Physician Aid in Dying," p. 7.

6. Barbara Dority, "The Ultimate Civil Liberty," *Humanist*, July/August 1997, p. 20.

7. Dority, "The Ultimate Civil Liberty," p. 20.

8. Quoted in Libertarian Party press release.

9. Quoted in Dority, "'In the Hands of the People,'" p. 6.

10. Quoted in Uhlmann, *Last Rights?*, p. 87.

11. John Shelby Spong, "On Assisted Suicide: Congressional Testimony," *Voice*, June 1996. www.dfms.org/newark/vox20696.html.

"Individuals can never have the right to commit a wrongful act, even upon themselves."

Individuals Do Not Have a Right to Die

"Few rallying cries sound more straightforward than the 'right to die'—but few are more fuzzy or misunderstood,"[1] writes law professor Yale Kamisar. Since death is inevitable, the notion of a right to die is strange. As one author notes, the concept "has a preposterous quality, conjuring up images of the state denying us that right and granting us immortality."[2] Adding to the confusion is the fact that the phrase has come to mean something different than when it was first coined. Originally, and somewhat misleadingly, it meant the right to be free of unwanted medical treatments at the end of life. This right was formally recognized by the U.S. Supreme Court in 1990.

However, it is inappropriate to think of the right to refuse medical treatment as a right to die. As physician Leon R. Kass explains, the right to refuse medical treatment "is properly seen not as part of a right to become dead but rather as part of a *right protecting how we choose to live*, even while we are dying."[3] It is important to understand this distinction because the phrase *right to die* is most often used in reference to physician-assisted suicide, in which a doctor provides a patient with lethal medication, or euthanasia, in which one person actively causes the death of another in order to relieve that person's suffering. In either context, the right to die does not exist.

No Right to Suicide

Sometimes people use *right to die* to mean a supposed right to commit suicide. Individuals have no such right. It is true that individuals have the *power* to commit suicide, and it is tragic when they do; however, this is not the same thing as having a *right* to suicide. Just because one can do something doesn't mean one should, and it certainly doesn't mean that one has a moral right to do so.

Those who claim that individuals should have the right to do whatever they please reveal a profound misunderstanding of the concept of rights. An individual's rights are grounded in a basic understanding of what types of acts are right and what are wrong. With rights come responsibilities: Individuals can never have the right to commit a wrongful act, even upon themselves. Professor Hadley V. Arkes explains that America's founders understood why individual freedom must be limited in this way, so they adopted the concept of "unalienable rights":

> "Unalienable rights" referred to the rights that we were not competent to alienate or waive, even for ourselves, because their goodness or badness was grounded in principle, quite independent of our will. And therefore, the Founders could understand that we may not properly alienate our freedom, or contract ourselves into slavery. And if we could not alienate our freedom, it went without saying that we could not alienate our own right, or obligation, to preserve our own lives.[4]

Suicide takes away a person's liberty; thus, a right to suicide is not compatible with the principles of freedom and responsibility upon which the United States was founded.

The Right to Die Is Really a Right to Kill

Most people, when they speak about a right to die, mean not just a right to suicide but also to physician-assisted suicide and euthanasia. These are not just matters of individual rights at all, since assisted suicide and euthanasia involve more than one person. They entail letting one person facilitate the death of another. As the International Anti-Euthanasia Task Force (IAETF) states,

> Euthanasia is not about giving rights to the person who dies but, instead, is about changing the law and public policy so that doctors, relatives and others can directly and intentionally end another person's life. This change would not give rights to the person who is killed, but to the person who does the killing.

"In other words," warns the IAETF, "euthanasia is not about the right to die. It's about the right to kill."[5]

From a legal and moral perspective, a right to kill is even more wrong than a right to suicide. But there are also practical concerns about a right to kill that also make it more dan-

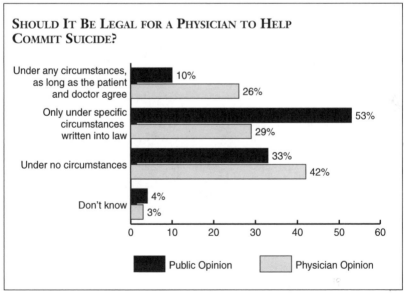

SHOULD IT BE LEGAL FOR A PHYSICIAN TO HELP COMMIT SUICIDE?

Source: AMA Opinion Survey, 1995

gerous. Not only would it turn both the legal system and the medical profession upside down if physicians had the right to kill their patients, but such a right would also be abused as doctors killed patients without their explicit consent. Medical care can be expensive, whereas physician-assisted death is not. It would endanger lives if this country were to recognize a right to die when the government has not even recognized a person's right to adequate health care.

An Unlimited Right

Advocates of euthanasia say the practice would be limited to terminally ill patients, but their preoccupation with individual rights belies the truth of that claim. If the Supreme Court were to decide that terminally ill patients have a right to die, non-terminally ill individuals would also eventually demand that right. As one observer notes, "If something's a fundamental right, then it's a fundamental right; it should be available to everybody in virtually all circumstances."[6] If terminally ill patients are granted the right to euthanasia, the government will be unable to justify denying this right to other suffering individuals—everyone from disabled persons to depressed teenagers would soon be entitled to euthanasia on demand.

Judicial Sleight of Hand

Despite these overwhelming arguments, two of the nation's highest courts recently ruled that individuals have a right to physician-assisted suicide. In March 1996 the U.S. Court of Appeals for the Ninth Circuit struck down a law in Washington State that barred doctors from assisting in suicides. A month later, the U.S. Court of Appeals for the Second Circuit struck down a similar law in New York. Both courts ruled that the state laws were unconstitutional—that is, that bans on assisted suicide violate a constitutionally protected right to die.

Both rulings were based on faulty logic and a shaky analysis of the Constitution. For example, the Ninth Circuit based its decision largely on the supposed right to privacy found in the Fourteenth Amendment. The Fourteenth Amendment emphasizes that the state shall not "deprive any citizen of life, liberty, or property without due process of law," and in past cases the Supreme Court has interpreted this to mean that the government should not intrude on people's intimate, private decisions. This right to privacy was summed up by the Court in the 1992 abortion case *Planned Parenthood v. Casey:*

> These matters, including the most intimate and per-
> sonal choices a person may make in a lifetime, choic-
> es central to personal dignity and autonomy, are
> central to the liberty protected by the Fourteenth
> Amendment. At the heart of liberty is the right to
> define one's own concept of existence, of meaning,
> of the universe, and of the mystery of human life. [7]

The Ninth Circuit concluded that euthanasia was such a decision—that euthanasia, like abortion, is a matter "central to one's own concept of existence." But this phrase is so vague that it could be used to encompass almost any decision a person might make. Clearly this passage, which invokes such intangibles as "the mystery of human life," is a poor justification for allowing doctors to give lethal medication to suicidal patients.

In addition to generalizing and distorting what the Constitution really says, both the Second and Ninth Circuits confused the different types of rights to die. Both courts ruled that, because the Supreme Court had already recognized a patient's right to refuse treatment, it had recognized a right to hasten one's own death and thus a right to assisted suicide. By equating the refusal of unwanted treatment with assistance in suicide, these courts confused the real issues. Only through such clever, almost devious tactics were these courts able to make a claim that the Constitution protects a right to assisted suicide.

The Supreme Court Sets the Record Straight

In March 1997 the Supreme Court reined in the overly creative judges of the Second and Ninth Circuits. The Supreme Court overturned both decisions of the lower courts, ruling that laws against assisted suicide are not unconstitutional. This ruling signifies a recognition by the Court that, although a limited right to privacy may exist, it does not justify an "anything goes" mentality. Individuals in a free society do not have the right to engage in any behavior they deem appropriate. Laws that discourage suicide and prohibit killing benefit the vast majority of people. They should not be abandoned just because a few individuals believe they are somehow entitled to euthanasia.

1. Yale Kamisar, "It Started with Quinlan: The Ever Expanding 'Right to Die,'" *Los Angeles Times*, March 31, 1996, p. M2.

2. Herbert Hendin, *Seduced by Death: Doctors, Patients, and the Dutch Cure*. New York: W.W. Norton, 1997, p. 157.

3. Leon R. Kass, "Dehumanization Triumphant," *First Things*, August/September 1996, p. 16.

4. Quoted in Michael M. Uhlmann, ed., *Last Rights?: Assisted Suicide and Euthanasia Debated*. Grand Rapids, MI: William B. Eerdmans, 1998, p. 97.

5. International Anti-Euthanasia Task Force, "Euthanasia: Answers to Frequently Asked Questions." www.iaetf.org/faq.htm.

6. David R. Carlin Jr., "Microscopic Rights: An Expanding Constitutional Universe," *Commonweal*, June 14, 1996, p. 8.

7. Quoted in Michael M. Uhlmann, "The Legal Logic of Euthanasia," *First Things*, June/July 1996, p. 40.

"The society that embraces euthanasia, even the 'mildest' and most 'voluntary' forms of it, tells people: 'We wouldn't mind getting rid of you.'"

Legalizing Euthanasia Would Harm Patients

Some people face great pain and suffering at the end of their lives. In such highly emotional situations, euthanasia may seem like an ethical and humane option. But in discussing the legalization of euthanasia, the issue is not simply what seems best for some patients but what would be best for society as a whole. Ezekiel Emanuel, a professor at Harvard Medical School, explains this distinction: "The question confronting the United States is one of policy: Should we broadly legalize physician-assisted suicide and euthanasia? We must not be swayed by a few—or even a thousand—wrenching cases in which such intervention seems unequivocally right."[1]

Depression and Suicide

Contrary to popular belief, most patients who seek euthanasia are not motivated by physical pain. Instead, psychological factors—often depression—are the cause of their suicidal tendencies. In the Netherlands, where euthanasia is a widely accepted practice, studies by the Dutch government reveal that pain is a motivating factor in less than half of all euthanasia cases. American studies support these findings. According to Emanuel,

The current euthanasia debate has been carried on in almost total ignorance of the facts and data available. The chief justification for considering euthanasia is to provide relief for patients suffering excruciating pain. But these patients are not the ones who want euthanasia. Depression, hopelessness, anxiety and the like are why patients request aid in dying.[2]

Many suicide attempts are really a depressed person's cry for help. Suicidal individuals often do not sincerely wish to die, and with psychological assistance they can overcome their depression. As Herbert Hendin, executive director of the American Suicide Foundation, points out, "Three-fourths of all suicides communicate their intentions, often with the hope that something will be done to make their suicide unnecessary."[3] However, if euthanasia is a legal right, doctors and family members will feel that they ought to quickly comply with a patient or loved one's request to die rather than thoroughly checking to see if the request is rational. Moreover, if assisted suicide becomes legal, depressed people will become even more likely to consider suicide as an option.

A Terrible Message

"An attempt at suicide," notes the National Right to Life Committee's department of biomedical ethics, "is often a challenge to see if anyone out there really cares."[4] The legalization of euthanasia or physician-assisted suicide would be a horrible answer to this challenge. It would send a devastating message not only to suicidal persons but also to anyone who has become weak or dependent on others because of illness or old age. As one author explains,

Instead of the message a humane society sends to its members—"Everybody has the right to be around, we want to keep you with us, every one of you"—the society that embraces euthanasia, even the "mildest" and most "voluntary" forms of it, tells people: "We wouldn't mind getting rid of you." This message reaches not only the elderly and the sick, but all the weak and dependent.[5]

Disadvantaged persons' fears that they are unwanted would be confirmed in the worst possible way. This is not a policy that America should take toward the elderly and the infirm.

A Duty to Die?

Because people often (mistakenly) associate what is legally permissible with what is morally correct, the legalization of euthanasia would profoundly change the way Americans think about death and dying. With the traditional taboo against killing gone, people would slowly come to accept euthanasia as normal. Doctors would become comfortable with assisted suicide as a routine treatment option. This normalization of assisted suicide would have a tragic impact on the way dying patients are treated.

Right-to-die activists say that euthanasia and assisted suicide would be completely voluntary, but there is no way to control the subtle coercions that can influence such decisions. Extremely ill patients, already worried that they are a burden to their families, would be pressured into choosing death. Herbert Hendin describes how this would occur: "A doctor who suggests euthanasia as an option to a patient . . . or relatives who respond too readily to a patient's mention of euthanasia send a powerful message that they believe that the patient should not continue to live."[6] The right to die would be perceived as a duty to die.

Pain Can Be Treated

Although most euthanasia requests are motivated by depression or other emotional problems, many individuals do suffer extreme physical pain at the end of life. Right-to-die activists would have such people believe that death is the only way to avoid such a painful existence. In painting such a grim picture, proponents of euthanasia ignore the hospice movement and the tremendous advances it has made in the treatment of pain.

Hospice care emerged in the 1970s when groups like the National Hospice Organization were formed "in response to the unmet needs of dying patients and their families for whom traditional medical care was no longer effective, appropriate, or desired."[7] Hospice professionals do not focus on curing disease and neither hasten nor postpone death. Instead, nurses, physicians, social workers, and dietitians do everything possible to improve the dying patient's final days. Hospice physicians and nurses emphasize pain management and palliative, or comfort, care. Such care often takes place in the patient's home rather than in a hospital.

According to hospice physician Ira Byock, "The best hospice and palliative-care programs have demonstrated that pain and physical suffering can *always* be alleviated."[8] Hospice caregivers commonly find that "once the pain and symptoms of an illness are under control, people rarely talk about taking their own lives."[9] If patients had better access to hospice care, and if doctors were better trained in techniques of pain man-

Mike Benson. Reprinted by special permission from United Features Syndicate.

agement, Americans would not be debating the legalization of physician-assisted suicide because they would not fear a painful, lonely death. "Instead of arguing whether assisted suicide should be legal or illegal," writes Byock, "let's do what is needed to make it irrelevant."[10]

Blaming the Sick for Their Suffering

Unfortunately, only 15 percent of Americans who died in 1996 were being treated with hospice care. Few Americans are even aware that this relatively new field of medicine exists. Too many dying patients are not offered the hospice option as it is, but according to Emanuel, if assisted suicide becomes legal, there will be far less incentive to comfort dying patients:

> Rather than being seen primarily as the victims of pain and suffering caused by disease, patients would be seen as having the power to end their suffering by agreeing to an injection or taking some pills; refusing would mean that living through the pain was the patient's decision, the patient's responsibility. Placing the blame on the patient would reduce the motivation of caregivers to provide the extra care that might be required.[11]

These feelings would have a tragic impact on the way society regards the terminally ill.

This concern is compounded by the fact that it would be easier and cheaper for health care plans to provide assisted suicide than to provide around-the-clock comfort care for days or weeks. "Just imagine the money that can be saved," writes euthanasia opponent Wesley J. Smith, "by not treating AIDS patients, or cancer patients, or people with physical disabilities, because they have been chosen or coerced into choosing an early exit."[12] After taking these financial concerns into account, it becomes clear that right-to-die advocates, whose supposed goal is to benefit terminally ill patients, have their priorities wrong. Patients would benefit most if the government would recognize their right to adequate health care, including hospice care. "Only *after* this right has been established does it make sense for courts to turn their attention to . . . physician-assisted suicide or euthanasia,"[13] concludes M. Scott Peck, author of *Denial of the Soul: Spiritual and Medical Perspectives on Euthanasia.*

More Harm than Good

If euthanasia becomes legal, it will affect more than just a few individuals—it will harm society as a whole. Legalization would result in the deaths of people who do not truly want to die—people who are depressed or who have requested euthanasia only because a doctor or family members have told them they should. Those dying patients who are in great physical pain need better access to hospice care, not euthanasia. Sanctioning physician-assisted death, even in limited circumstances, simply poses too great a threat to patients.

1. Ezekiel Emanuel, "Whose Right to Die?" *Atlantic Monthly*, March 1997, p. 78.

2. Ezekiel Emanuel, "The Painful Truth About Euthanasia," *Wall Street Journal*, January 7, 1997, p. A18.

3. Herbert Hendin, *Seduced by Death: Doctors, Patients, and the Dutch Cure.* New York: W.W. Norton, 1997, p. 156.

4. Burke J. Balch and Randall K. O'Bannon, "Why We Shouldn't Legalize Assisted Suicide, Part I: Suicide and Mental Illness." www.nrlc.org/euthanasia/asisuid1.html.

5. Quoted in New York State Task Force on Life and the Law, *When Death Is Sought: Assisted Suicide and Euthanasia in the Medical Context.* New York State Department of Health, May 1994, p. 102. www.health.state.ny.us/nysdoh/provider/death.htm.

6. Hendin, *Seduced by Death*, p. 157.

7. National Hospice Organization, "Statement of the National Hospice Organization Opposing the Legalization of Euthanasia and Assisted Suicide," 1997. www.nho.org/pasposition.htm.

8. Quoted in Joe Loconte, "Hospice, Not Hemlock," *Policy Review*, March/April 1998, p. 45.

9. Loconte, "Hospice, Not Hemlock," p. 44.

10. Ira Byock, "Why Do We Make Dying So Miserable?" *Washington Post*, January 22, 1997. www.afsp.org/assisted/byock.htm.

11. Emanuel, "Whose Right to Die?" p. 79.

12. Wesley J. Smith, "Demanding Death-on-Demand," *Heterodoxy*, May/June 1996, p. 14.

13. M. Scott Peck, "Living Is the Mystery," *Newsweek*, March 10, 1997, p. 18.

"Doctors and patients should be able to openly discuss euthanasia without the fear that they are committing a crime."

Legalizing Euthanasia Would Benefit Patients

Many people are afraid they will die a lingering, painful death, and with good reason. People today are more likely to suffer from a slow death caused by chronic, debilitating diseases such as cancer and heart disease than ever before. Right-to-die activist Barbara Coombs Lee sums up the problem: "Medical science has conquered the gentle and peaceful deaths and left the humiliating and agonizing to run their relentless downhill course."[1] "The crisis is real," writes hospice physician Ira Byock. "Studies document that pain among the terminally ill is widespread and undertreated, even within our most prestigious medical centers."[2]

"Dressing Up Hospice Care as a Panacea"

Dr. Byock advocates hospice care as an alternative to physician-assisted suicide or euthanasia. No one disputes the idea that doctors have a responsibility to do everything possible to relieve the suffering of dying patients, or that dying patients should have better access to hospice care. In its position statement on hospice care, the Hemlock Society, whose goal is the legalization of voluntary euthanasia, states: "We really admire hospice's ability to provide compassionate care, alleviate much of the suffering and pain of terminal illness, and to deal with the spiritual and psychological concerns of the patient and the family. We agree that when these concerns are handled, many people who would want to end their lives change their minds."[3]

Yet there are several points on which people in the right-to-die movement and some hospice advocates disagree. For example, Byock makes the claim that "pain can always be alleviated."[4] This is simply an exaggeration. As hospice physician Timothy E. Quill states, "There are inherent limitations to hospice care. We are good at relieving suffering on hospice, but not 100% of the time. We must learn to acknowledge the exceptions."[5] Still another hospice physician states that "dressing up hospice care as a panacea, and the only moral alternative to physician-assisted suicide, is unhelpful and inaccurate."[6]

Hospice or Hemlock: A Decision for the Patient

Even if hospice care could relieve all patients' pain, many studies have indicated that pain is often not the sole motivating factor behind a person's request to die. According to the Hemlock Society, "The most frightening aspect of death for many is not physical pain, but the prospect of losing control and independence and of dying in an undignified, unaesthetic, absurd, and existentially unacceptable condition."[7] Some patients consider dependency, immobility, and the loss of control over bodily functions and mental faculties to be worse than physical pain. And the very drugs that hospice physicians use to relieve physical pain may induce these symptoms.

Hospice care cannot obviate the need for legalized physician-assisted dying, and patients should not be forced to choose one or the other. Both options are for the benefit of dying patients, so both should be available to them. Timothy E. Quill, who is both a hospice physician and a leading advocate of a patient's right to choose a dignified death, sums up how the two philosophies are compatible: "Physician-assisted suicide is a narrow question to be raised only when good palliative care fails."[8]

Fears About Abuse

Aware that hospice care cannot really preclude the need for euthanasia, opponents of physician-assisted dying often choose a different tactic. They claim that, if legalized, the practice will become widespread and might be applied inappropriately. The Oregon Death with Dignity Act provides a good model for how these concerns can be addressed. Among its many safeguards are requirements that the patient be mentally competent, that his or her request be thoroughly documented, and that two independent physicians verify the patient's diagnosis with a terminal illness. In the first year that it was legal in Oregon, few people chose assisted suicide. Only fifteen of the twenty-nine thousand deaths that occurred in Oregon in 1998 were officially sanctioned physician-assisted suicides.

Despite all the safeguards against it, there is still the possibility that family members or doctors might try to influence patients' choices concerning assisted suicide. But as euthanasia activist Barbara Dority explains,

> No law can ultimately guarantee that coercion will never occur. Likewise, there is no guarantee that all forms of coercion have been eliminated from a host of other life decisions and situations. . . . But shall we curtail our available choices because we don't believe people can always make them for the right reasons or because we fear possible abuses?[9]

Doctors and lawmakers should do everything possible to prevent abuses, but it would be wrong to deny the option to everyone based solely on speculations that they might occur. With freedom comes responsibility.

The Current Situation Is Worse

In fact, abuses are more likely to occur in the current environment. Doctors have always helped suffering patients by hastening their deaths. One way that physicians are able to covertly perform euthanasia is through the practice of "terminal sedation." For patients in extreme pain, doctors are allowed to administer as much medication as necessary to relieve the pain. Morphine is most commonly used for this purpose; however, high doses of the drug can be lethal. The doctrine of double effect, a recognized principle of medical ethics, tells doctors that it is acceptable to administer morphine for pain control even if, as an unintended side effect, terminal sedation occurs and the patient dies.

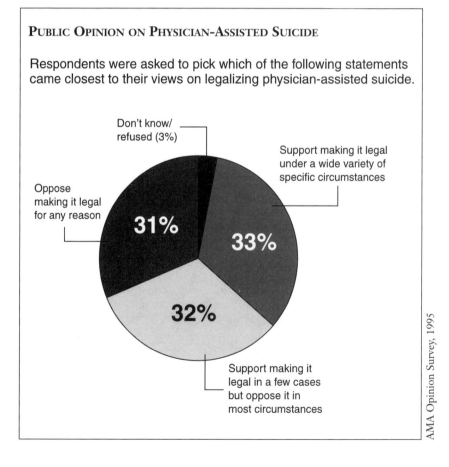

PUBLIC OPINION ON PHYSICIAN-ASSISTED SUICIDE

Respondents were asked to pick which of the following statements came closest to their views on legalizing physician-assisted suicide.

Don't know/ refused (3%)

Support making it legal under a wide variety of specific circumstances

Oppose making it legal for any reason

31%

33%

32%

Support making it legal in a few cases but oppose it in most circumstances

AMA Opinion Survey, 1995

The doctrine of double effect serves an important purpose: Without it, doctors would not prescribe adequate doses of medication for fear of being accused of killing their patients. Yet many doctors do use terminal sedation to kill patients when they request it, and then take legal refuge in the doctrine of double effect, saying they only intended to relieve pain. Physicians should not have to engage in this deception. Doctors and patients should be able to openly discuss euthanasia without the fear that they are committing a crime.

Because it occurs in secret, no one knows exactly how widespread covert euthanasia is, but certainly abuses are far easier to perpetrate than they would be if physician-assisted death was out in the open and subject to regulation. "There is no accountability for such deaths, no procedures, no safeguards, and no reporting requirements," writes Dority. "How much safer and more empowered all those involved would be if laws such as Oregon's . . . were in place nationwide."[10] In addition, says the Hemlock Society's Faye J. Girsh, "A mockery is made of the existing law,"[11] because juries routinely acquit persons like Jack Kevorkian who have helped people to die.

An Added Benefit

Legalizing physician aid in dying would benefit patients in another way as well. Many patients are not ready to die but want the assurance that they will be able to achieve a dignified death if their condition worsens. As one author explains,

> Permitting doctor-assisted suicide will actually prolong some patients' lives. What patients often want is not so much the ability to die but the knowledge that they have control over the timing of their death. Once such control is permitted, they may be more willing to undergo aggressive medical treatments that are painful and risky. If a treatment does not succeed but only worsens the patient's condition, the person is assured that he or she can end the suffering.[12]

This is already evident in Oregon—although fifteen people ended their lives with the help of a physician in 1998, an additional eight received prescriptions for lethal medication but chose not to use them. Again, this shows that euthanasia is about autonomy and patient control, not just fear of suffering. Far from showing a lack of respect for life, by legalizing voluntary euthanasia society would demonstrate respect for the decisions people make *about* their lives.

1. Quoted in House Committee on the Judiciary, Subcommittee on the Constitution, *Oversight Hearing: Assisted Suicide in the United States*, 104th Cong., 2nd sess., April 29, 1996. www.house.gov/judiciary/2173.htm.

2. Ira Byock, "Why Do We Make Dying So Miserable?" *Washington Post*, January 22, 1997. www.afsp.org/assisted/byock.htm.

3. Hemlock Society USA, "Hospice and Hemlock: A Position Statement." www2.privatei.com/hemlock/hospice.html.

4. Byock, "Why Do We Make Dying So Miserable?"

5. Quoted in John C. Fletcher, moderator, "Deciding About Death: Physician-Assisted Suicide and the Courts—a Panel Discussion," *Pharos*, Winter 1998, p. 3.

6. John L. Miller, "Hospice Care or Assisted Suicide: A False Dichotomy," *American Journal of Hospice and Palliative Care*, May/June 1997. http://www2.privatei.com/hemlock/hoscare.html.

7. Hemlock Society USA, "Hospice and Hemlock: A Position Statement."

8. Quoted in Fletcher, "Deciding About Death," p. 3.

9. Barbara Dority, "The Ultimate Civil Liberty," *Humanist*, July/August 1997, p. 18.

10. Dority, "The Ultimate Civil Liberty," p. 19.

11. Faye J. Girsh, "The Case for Physician Aid in Dying," *Journal of the Hippocratic Society*, Fall 1997, p. 10.

12. David Orentlicher, "Navigating the Narrows of Doctor-Assisted Suicide," *Technology Review*, July 1996, p. 63.

"Once the public is used to the notion that certain individuals are less than authentically human, the category of disposable people will relentlessly expand."

Legalized Euthanasia Would Lead to Involuntary Killing

When a society legally condones killing, even mercy killing, it is a sign that people in that society have begun to lose respect for human life. Once the first step down this slippery slope is taken, it is difficult to stop the downward slide. One physician explains how this occurs:

> Once legalized, physician-assisted suicide and euthanasia would become routine. Over time doctors would become comfortable giving injections to end life and Americans would become comfortable having euthanasia as an option. Comfort would make us want to extend the option to others who, in society's view, are suffering and leading purposeless lives.[1]

Those deemed to be suffering too much could include the disabled, the mentally ill, the poor—anyone whom the majority of physicians, ethicists, and lawmakers judge to have a low quality of life. This is the real danger of euthanasia: It will lead to widespread government-sanctioned mercy killing.

The American Experience with Abortion

Many people have trouble believing that euthanasia could ever become widespread, but few people in the early 1960s imagined that abortions would ever become as common as they are. Early on in the abortion controversy, many people assumed that abortion would only be used in cases of rape or incest—just as advocates of euthanasia now assure people that euthanasia will only be used in extreme circumstances. But as physician Leon R. Kass and attorney Nelson Lund note, "Massive numbers of abortions are now being performed, far beyond what was originally expected, and for reasons not originally regarded as appropriate."[2] People will become similarly desensitized if euthanasia is legalized. Americans are accustomed to getting rid of the unwanted at one end of life; they will eventually come to accept it at the other.

The Ever-Expanding Right to Die

There is no way that euthanasia can realistically be limited to the terminally ill. "Once the public is used to the notion that certain individuals are less than authentically human," writes *New American* senior editor William Norman Grigg, "the category of disposable people will relentlessly expand."[3] For example, some proponents of euthanasia argue that suffering persons who are not terminally ill are actually in greater need of euthanasia since their suffering is likely to last longer. It would be discrimination, other euthanasia activists contend, to allow a few patients the right to die but to deny a "humane" death to others. The same goes for nonvoluntary euthanasia, which is performed without the patient's consent: If physician-assisted death benefits suffering patients, then why should doctors deny this benefit to patients who cannot request it—for example, handicapped infants? This is the logic of the slippery slope, logic that can be used to kill people "for their own good."

Judging Human Worth

It is already clear that Americans would accept euthanasia for the depressed and the disabled. Jack Kevorkian, the doctor who kills his patients, has admitted to assisting in over one hundred deaths. But Wesley J. Smith, a staunch euthanasia opponent, points out that "approximately 80 percent of Kevorkian's victims were *not* terminally ill. Most of them have been people with disabilities, primarily multiple sclerosis but also arthritis and spinal-cord injury."[4] Americans have condoned Kevorkian's behavior—and acquitted him of murder several times—because far too many people believe that the lives of disabled people are worth less than those of others.

The Holocaust is history's most infamous example of how this belief can be used to justify atrocity. Right-to-die activists think it is preposterous to compare the "compassionate" killing of suffering persons to the slaughter of 6 million Jews during World War II. But the Holocaust was preceded in Nazi Germany by a euthanasia program in which the mentally and physically handicapped were painlessly killed. Once the Nazis had accepted that people of a certain health status should be "helped to die," the groundwork was laid for the idea that people from a specific ethnic background should also be killed. Obviously, Americans today possess a sense of justice that prevents them from condoning genocide. But to preserve this sense of justice, Americans must learn from history and not sanction killing that is motivated by a perverse sense of compassion.

Freeing Up Scarce Resources

Hitler's euthanasia program for the mentally ill and the disabled was motivated in part by a need to free up hospital beds for wounded soldiers. Similar motives may taint the modern right-to-die movement. Caring for the sick, the elderly, and the disabled can be incredibly expensive. Medicare, the government health insurance program for Americans over age sixty-five, spends nearly 30 percent of its budget on patients in their final year of life. Physician-assisted suicide would certainly be a cheaper way to deal with such expensive drains on the nation's economy.

In addition, more than 60 million Americans are enrolled in health maintenance organizations, or HMOs. In this type of health plan, members pay one monthly premium for coverage, regardless of how much or how little health care they use. To make a profit, HMOs must restrict the amount of money they spend on each patient's health care. HMO doctors are encouraged to ration health care and recommend only the most inexpensive treatments. Of course, euthanasia would be the cheapest treatment of all. "If euthanasia is legalized," writes Smith, "Wall Street investors who invest in for-profit HMOs will be dancing in the streets."[5]

Not only do right-to-die advocates acknowledge the financial incentive to killing off expensive patients, but some even think the potential savings are a good reason for patients to choose death. "There is no contradicting the fact that since the largest medical expenses are incurred in the final days and weeks of life, the hastened demise of people with only a short time left would free resources for others,"[6] write Hemlock Society founder Derek Humphry and attorney Mary Clement. Ethicist John Hardwig believes that, as people become less useful to society and more of a financial burden, they gradually develop a "duty to die":

> A duty to die is more likely when continuing to live will impose significant burdens—emotional burdens, extensive caregiving, destruction of life plans, and yes, financial hardship—on your family and loved ones. . . . A duty to die becomes greater as you grow older. . . . There is less likely to be a duty to die if you can still make significant contributions to the lives of others.[7]

The logic of euthanasia leads to such situations. By accepting that some lives are not worth living, society promotes the idea that not all lives have value.

Euthanasia proponents blithely dismiss concerns that euthanasia might be forced on people, claiming that it would be strictly regulated to prevent abuse. The problem is that the proposed safeguards would be woefully inadequate. A former supporter of euthanasia, physician Diane E. Meier writes that "rules would be difficult, if not impossible, to enforce." For example, she points out, the requirement that dying patients be mentally alert when they request euthanasia would rarely be met: "Intermittent confusion, anxiety and depression [among terminally ill patients] are the rule rather than the exception, inevitably clouding judgement."[8]

Involuntary Killing in the Netherlands

Evidence that such safeguards are ineffective can be found in the Netherlands, where euthanasia remains technically illegal but has been practiced openly for years. "Virtually every guideline established by the Dutch to regulate euthanasia has been modified or violated with impunity," says Herbert Hendin, executive director of the American Suicide Foundation: "Legal sanction creates a permissive atmosphere which seems to foster not taking the guidelines too seriously."[9] In one 1994 case, a psychiatrist assisted in the suicide of a woman whose only malady was that she was grief-stricken over the death of her two sons. The psychiatrist was acquitted by a Dutch court, and his license was not even suspended.

Dutch doctors have become comfortable deciding whether their patients would be better off dead. This was tragically confirmed in 1992 when a study commissioned by the Dutch government revealed that in more than one thousand cases each year, euthanasia occurred without the patient's request. Right-to-die activists once touted the Netherlands as a model of how euthanasia could be regulated effectively; now it is an undeniable example of the abuse that occurs when a society sanctions mercy killing.

In the span of roughly thirty years, America has moved from legalizing passive euthanasia for comatose patients to debating whether doctors should help terminally ill patients commit suicide (and this practice has been legalized in

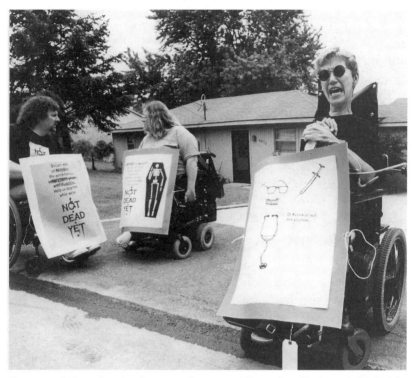

Some people fear that legalizing euthanasia will put the elderly and the handi-capped in jeopardy of premature death. Here, activists from the disabled rights group Not Dead Yet sit outside of Jack Kevorkian's home to protest the fact that many of the patients he has helped to die have been disabled rather than termi-nally ill.

Oregon). The Netherlands, decades ahead of the United States in its progress down the slippery slope, has already moved from physician-assisted suicide to active euthanasia and finally to the involuntary killing of over one thousand of its citizens per year. The experience of the Netherlands should serve as a grave warning to Americans. The United States must reverse its slide down the slippery slope by insti-tuting a federal ban on physician-assisted suicide and active euthanasia.

1. Ezekiel Emanuel, "Whose Right to Die?" *Atlantic Monthly*, March 1997, p. 79.

2. Leon R. Kass and Nelson Lund, "Courting Death: Assisted Suicide, Doctors, and the Law," *Commentary*, December 1996, p. 20.

3. William Norman Grigg, "Abortion and Beyond," *New American*, January 19, 1998, p. 17.

4. Wesley J. Smith, "The Serial Killer as Folk Hero," *Weekly Standard*, July 13, 1998, p. 11.

5. Wesley J. Smith, "Demanding Death-on-Demand," *Heterodoxy*, May/June 1996, p. 14.

6. Derek Humphry and Mary Clement, *Freedom to Die: People, Politics, and the Right-to-Die Movement*. New York: St. Martin's, 1998, p. 333.

7. John Hardwig, "Is There a Duty to Die?" *Hastings Center Report*, March/April 1997, pp. 38–39.

8. Diane E. Meier, "A Change of Heart on Assisted Suicide," *New York Times*, April 24, 1998. www.afsp.assisted/meier.htm.

9. Herbert Hendin, *Seduced by Death: Doctors, Patients, and the Dutch Cure*. New York: W.W. Norton, 1997, p. 23.

"[Physician-assisted dying] is not a nightmarish notion conjured up by some depraved group of people; it is a response to deep concerns for human well-being and human rights."

Legalized Euthanasia Would Not Lead to Involuntary Killing

Slippery slope arguments essentially propose that any change to the way things are will have the most disastrous consequences possible. Moreover, because the "slope" that society has slid down is so "slippery," it will not be possible to set things back to the way they were once things go wrong. To avoid this imagined slope, then, society must not risk instituting any new reforms at all. But this is exactly the problem with slippery slope arguments: They are always used as an unwavering defense of the status quo.

Nightmarish Scenarios

So it is with euthanasia. Slippery slope arguments against euthanasia hold that if voluntary, physician-assisted suicide is allowed in certain cases, it will inevitably be allowed in cases that are not as clear-cut, and eventually there will be an unstoppable army of euthanasia-happy doctors running the nation's hospitals. Once terminally ill patients are allowed access to assisted suicide, the argument goes, no amount of vigilance can prevent the ensuing bloodshed. Women, the disabled, the poor, the elderly, and any number of minority groups will become victims of forced euthanasia, or so Americans are told.

If this scenario sounds alarmist, that's because it is. Slippery slope arguments are designed to play on people's fears. But where is the evidence that such nightmarish scenarios are unavoidable? Why must euthanasia for those who want to die inevitably lead to euthanasia for those who do not if there is a clear law that requires the patient to request it multiple times and in the presence of witnesses? How can euthanasia for the terminally ill be transformed into euthanasia for people who are not dying if the law clearly requires such a diagnosis from a doctor?

Nazi Germany

Opponents of euthanasia sometimes offer the example of Nazi Germany as validation of the slippery slope theory. It is true that, in addition to practicing genocide against Jews and other minorities, the Nazis supported euthanasia, and in September 1939 Hitler did issue a secret decree in which he ordered the involuntary killing of the incurably insane, the handicapped, and others whom he referred to as "useless eaters."

But just because the Nazis sanctioned murder under the name *euthanasia* is not evidence that legalizing widespread euthanasia would lead to genocide. As philosopher Daniel Callahan explains, "The Nazi experience is only partially relevant. Theirs was not a move from legal voluntary euthanasia to involuntary killing. They never had the first phase at all, but went straight to the killing."[1] Author Stephen Jamison says the Nazi euthanasia programs "were designed from above with the intention from the very beginning of gradually creating a system of genocide rooted in the concept of racial purity."[2] They were rooted in hatred and anti-Semitism, not compassion.

There are also very important differences between modern America and World War II Germany. Most importantly, notes right-to-die activist Gerald A. Larue, is that "what took place in Germany occurred under a dictatorship, not in a democratic setting."[3] "The true slippery slope in Nazi Germany," writes Jamison, "was the loss of civil liberty and freedoms. By contrast, the current call for legalizing physician-assisted dying is rooted in the concept of choice for the individual."[4] The right-to-die movement is based on respect for the individual, not a desire to kill.

The Dutch Experience with Euthanasia

Comparisons between the modern right-to-die movement and the Holocaust are extreme, alarmist, and ultimately unfounded. A more realistic example of how legally sanctioned euthanasia affects society can be found in the Netherlands. Euthanasia remains formally illegal there, but since the late 1970s the Dutch courts have not prosecuted doctors for performing euthanasia if they follow certain guidelines, the most important of which is that the patient makes a well-considered, voluntary request for aid in dying.

The Dutch have permitted euthanasia not because they believe people ought to end their lives but because they have chosen not to ignore the suffering that dying patients endure. "The euthanasia debate is far from over here," says Dutch professor of social medicine Gerrit van der Waal, "but there is acceptance of the phenomenon. There's less discussion of the pros and cons, and more about how to control it."[5] Dutch doctors and citizens have not become desensitized to the moral ramifications of euthanasia—"It's still as emotional and difficult as ever,"[6] says Bert Keizer, a physician at a nursing home in Amsterdam.

Although it has been openly practiced in the Netherlands for over twenty years, less than 3 percent of deaths in the Netherlands occur with the help of a physician. Most requests for euthanasia are turned away, and over 80 percent of those who do receive euthanasia have cancer. Most of these individuals have less than a month to live. The widespread killing predicted by the slippery slope theory has not occurred.

Acknowledging Problems Rather than Ignoring Them

Still, there have been some abuses. The Remmelink Report, a government-commissioned study of euthanasia, reported that about one thousand people per year in the Netherlands are euthanized without explicitly asking for it. And there are individual cases of doctors who have acceded too quickly to patients' requests. These cases are in no way excusable, but the Dutch should not be condemned for openly acknowledging them. "Doctors all over the world shorten the lives of patients," says Keizer, "and only we [in the Netherlands] are stupid enough to talk about it."[7] Euthanasia and its associated abuses occur in every country. The Dutch realized this fact; that is one reason why they chose to regulate the practice. Because Americans choose to pretend that such abuses do not exist, the U.S. government has no idea how many doctors—like Jack Kevorkian, for example—are secretly performing euthanasia without any supervision whatsoever.

But America need not follow exactly in the footsteps of the Dutch, either. For example, the Dutch euthanasia guidelines do not distinguish between active euthanasia and physician-assisted suicide; American law would only allow physician-assisted suicide because it ensures the patient's control over the process. Likewise, the Dutch do not limit euthanasia to the terminally ill; American safeguards would require a doctor to confirm that the patient's death is already imminent.

A Limited Right to Die

Legalized physician-assisted suicide in America would not be like euthanasia in the Netherlands for another reason: Unlike the Netherlands, the United States does not guarantee its citizens access to adequate health care. In Holland, no one worries about how they will pay for their health care, and most people know and trust their family doctor. The American health care system, however, is becoming increasingly impersonal and cost conscious. There is the real risk that poor Americans, or those who require expensive care, might be pressured into euthanasia. This is precisely why all proposals to legalize physician-assisted suicide limit it to the terminally ill.

In theory, all suffering persons, not just the terminally ill, should be entitled to a dignified death at the time of their choosing. However, this does not mean, as opponents have charged, that right-to-die activists have a hidden agenda to eventually expand euthanasia beyond current proposals. The potential for abuse is real, and so there must be limits and safeguards on what types of euthanasia are allowed. "There would be no progression beyond what is publicly dictated," says the Hemlock Society's Faye J. Girsh:

> Terminally ill, mentally competent adults is the category of individuals we are generally talking about now, although some proposals have included people with hopeless illnesses. We have not had a chance to see how this model of physician aid in dying will work; it is premature to consider expanding the law at this point.[8]

The Slippery Slope Is Both Unlikely and Preventable

Physician-assisted dying, as Larue explains, "is not a nightmarish notion conjured up by some depraved group of people; it is a response to deep concerns for human well-being and human rights."[9] Americans will not permit involuntary killing as the Nazis did, and safeguards can prevent the types of abuses that have occurred in the Netherlands. It is impossible to deny that mistakes might be made once assisted suicide is legalized and regulated, but it is wrong to pretend that such abuses do not occur already. One group of doctors sums up the current situation: "Physician-assisted suicide currently occurs in secret, without publicly sanctioned criteria and without any independent scrutiny. . . . The legal status quo regarding physician-assisted death does not adequately serve the needs of dying patients with unrelievable suffering."[10] Unfounded slippery slope arguments make a poor defense for this status quo.

1. Quoted in Gerald A. Larue, *Playing God: Fifty Religions' Views on Your Right to Die.* Wakefield, RI: Moyer Bell, 1996, p. 27.

2. Stephen Jamison, *Final Acts of Love: Families, Friends, and Assisted Dying.* New York: G.P. Putnam's Sons, 1995, p. 255.

3. Larue, *Playing God*, p. 25.

4. Jamison, *Final Acts of Love*, p. 255.

5. Quoted in Barbara Smit, "I Want to Draw the Line Myself," *Time*, March 17, 1997, p. 30.

6. Quoted in Smit, "I Want to Draw the Line Myself," p. 31.

7. Quoted in Smit, "I Want to Draw the Line Myself," p. 31.

8. Faye J. Girsh, "The Case for Physician Aid in Dying," *Journal of the Hippocratic Society*, Fall 1997, p. 9.

9. Larue, *Playing God*, p. 22.

10. Franklin G. Miller et al., "Regulating Physician-Assisted Death," *New England Journal of Medicine*, July 14, 1994, p. 119.

Appendix A

Facts About Euthanasia

Caring for the Dying

- Every year 2 million people die in America, 80 percent in hospitals, hospices, or nursing homes. Chronic illness, such as cancer or heart disease, accounts for 2 of every 3 deaths. It is estimated that approximately 70 percent of these people die after a decision is made to forgo life-sustaining treatment.
- Medicare, the government health insurance program for Americans over age 65, spends approximately 30 percent of its budget on care for patients in their last year of life.
- Only 5 of the nation's 126 medical schools require courses in the care of the dying.
- A nationwide Gallup Survey conducted for the National Hospice Organization in fall 1996 indicated that 9 out of 10 adults would prefer to be cared for at home if they were terminally ill with 6 months or less to live. The majority of adults would be interested in a comprehensive program of care, such as hospice.
- Approximately 77 percent of hospice patients die at home.
- In 1994 Medicare spent $1.2 billion of its roughly $200 billion budget on hospice services.
- In 1995, 60 percent of hospice patients had cancer; 6 percent heart-related diagnoses; 4 percent had AIDS; 1 percent renal (kidney) diagnoses; 2 percent Alzheimer's; and 27 percent "other." In 1995, hospices cared for about 1 out of every 2 cancer deaths in America.
- There is no nationwide standard on what the cost of caring for a hospice patient is. The closest determination is Medicare per diem rates which for fiscal year 1997 were $94.17 per day for home care and $418.93 per day for general inpatient care.

The Legal Status of Euthanasia

- Active euthanasia, or mercy killing, is illegal in all 50 states.
- In November 1998 Michigan voters defeated a proposal to legalize physician-assisted suicide, with 71 percent of voters opposing the measure and 29 percent supporting it.
- In 1991 voters in Washington State rejected a ballot initiative to legalize physician-assisted suicide by a vote of 54 to 46 percent.
- In 1992 California voters also rejected a measure to legalize physician-assisted suicide by an identical margin of 54 to 46 percent.

- At least 20 state legislatures have considered and rejected bills to legalize assisted suicide.
- 35 states have laws that expressly criminalize euthanasia and physician-assisted suicide, while in 9 other states and the District of Columbia, helping someone to die is considered illegal based on legal precedents within the state. In Utah, Wyoming, Ohio, Virginia, and North Carolina, the legality of assisted suicide is unclear.

Physician-Assisted Suicide in Oregon

- On November 8, 1994, Oregon voters passed Ballot Measure 16, a physician-assisted suicide law, with 51 percent of voters supporting the measure and 49 percent opposing.
- The law was held up in the courts, and did not go into effect until November 4, 1997, when Oregonians rejected a measure to repeal the law by a vote of 60 percent to 40 percent. Assisted suicide is now officially legal in Oregon.
- In 1998, 23 people received prescriptions for lethal medication under Oregon's Death with Dignity Act. Information was only revealed for the 21 of these patients who died in 1998.
- Of those who died, 11 were men and 10 were women. All were white. Eighteen of the patients had cancer, while the other 3 had AIDS, a chronic lung condition, and congestive heart failure.
- 15 used their prescriptions while the other 6 died as a result of their illness.

National Surveys About Physician-Assisted Suicide

According to a national survey of physicians published in the April 23, 1998, *New England Journal of Medicine:*
- 11 percent of physicians said there are circumstances in which they would provide lethal medication to patients; 36 percent said they would prescribe such medication if it were legal to do so.
- 7 percent said that under certain circumstances they would administer a lethal injection to a patient; 24 percent said they would do so if the practice were legal.
- 18.3 percent of respondents said they had received requests from patients for lethal medications with which to commit suicide; 16 percent of the doctors who received such requests granted them.
- 4.7 percent of all the respondents had ever given a lethal injection to a patient.
- In every case of assisted suicide or euthanasia, the physician believed that the request reflected the patient's wishes.
- 95 percent of the requests for lethal medication came from the patients themselves; 54 percent of requests for a lethal injection came from the patient's family member or partner.

Jack Kevorkian

- Jack Kevorkian is a retired pathologist from Michigan who claims to have assisted in over 130 suicides (although not all of them have been confirmed). He has a medical degree, but the state of Michigan has revoked his license to practice medicine.
- The majority of persons that Kevorkian has helped to die have been female and not terminally ill.
- Prior to 1998, Kevorkian had been formally accused of murder or of assisting in suicide on 5 occasions, but each time he was either acquitted or the charges were dropped.
- In most cases, Kevorkian has assisted patients by hooking them up to his "suicide machine," by which they flip a switch to self-administer a lethal dose of medication intravenously.
- However, on November 22, 1998, CBS's *60 Minutes* showed a videotape of Kevorkian administering a lethal injection to Thomas Youk, a 52-year-old Michigan man with amyotrophic lateral sclerosis (Lou Gehrig's disease). The videotape showed Youk confirming that he was consenting to active euthanasia, as opposed to physician-assisted suicide. Kevorkian says he allowed the death to be televised in order to force prosecutors to arrest him and to generate debate over the distinctions between assisted suicide and active euthanasia.
- On March 26, 1999, a Michigan jury found Kevorkian guilty of both second-degree murder and delivery of a controlled substance. Unlike Kevorkian's previous trials, in this case the judge did not allow the defense to present testimony about Youk's pain and suffering, and emphasized that whether the victim consents is legally irrelevant in murder cases. Kevorkian faces up to 32 years in prison, but his lawyer, David Gorosh, says he will appeal.

APPENDIX B

Excerpts from Related Documents Pertaining to Euthanasia

Document 1: The Gospel of Life

The Roman Catholic Church is adamantly opposed to euthanasia, on the grounds that the intentional destruction of human life is always immoral. On March 25, 1995, Pope John Paul II issued the papal encyclical Evangelium Vitae, *or "The Gospel of Life," in which he articulated the church's opposition to both abortion and euthanasia—the acceptance of which he declared to be part of a growing "culture of death." Selected passages dealing with euthanasia are excerpted below.*

The deliberate decision to deprive an innocent human being of his life is always morally evil and can never be licit either as an end in itself or as a means to a good end. It is in fact a grave act of disobedience to the moral law, and indeed to God himself, the author and guarantor of that law; it contradicts the fundamental virtues of justice and charity. [The Church has stated:] "Nothing and no one can in any way permit the killing of an innocent human being, whether a fetus or an embryo, an infant or an adult, an old person, or one suffering from an incurable disease, or a person who is dying. Furthermore, no one is permitted to ask for this act of killing, either for himself or herself or for another person entrusted to his or her care, nor can he or she consent to it, either explicitly or implicitly. Nor can any authority legitimately recommend or permit such an action.". . .

Important Distinctions

Euthanasia must be distinguished from the decision to forego so-called "aggressive medical treatment," in other words, medical procedures which no longer correspond to the real situation of the patient, either because they are by now disproportionate to any expected results or because they impose an excessive burden on the patient and his family. In such situations, when death is clearly imminent and inevitable, one can in conscience "refuse forms of treatment that would only secure a precarious and burdensome prolongation of life, so long as the normal care due to the sick person in similar cases is not interrupted." Certainly there is a moral obligation to care for oneself and to allow oneself to be cared for, but this duty must take account of concrete circumstances. It needs to be determined whether the means of treatment available are objectively proportionate to the prospects for improvement. To forego extraordinary or disproportionate means is not the equivalent of suicide or euthanasia; it rather expresses acceptance of the human condition in the face of death. . . .

Taking into account these distinctions, in harmony with the Magisterium of my Predecessors and in communion with the Bishops of the Catholic Church, *I confirm that euthanasia is a grave violation of the law of*

God, since it is the deliberate and morally unacceptable killing of a human person. This doctrine is based upon the natural law and upon the written word of God, is transmitted by the Church's Tradition and taught by the ordinary and universal Magisterium.

Depending on the circumstances, this practice involves the malice proper to suicide or murder.

Suicide is always as morally objectionable as murder. The Church's tradition has always rejected it as a gravely evil choice. Even though a certain psychological, cultural and social conditioning may induce a person to carry out an action which so radically contradicts the innate inclination to life, thus lessening or removing subjective responsibility, *suicide*, when viewed objectively, is a gravely immoral act. In fact, it involves the rejection of love of self and the renunciation of the obligation of justice and charity towards one's neighbour, towards the communities to which one belongs, and towards society as a whole. In its deepest reality, suicide represents a rejection of God's absolute sovereignty over life and death, as proclaimed in the prayer of the ancient sage of Israel: "You have power over life and death; you lead men down to the gates of Hades and back again."

False Mercy

To concur with the intention of another person to commit suicide and to help in carrying it out through so-called "assisted suicide" means to cooperate in, and at times to be the actual perpetrator of, an injustice which can never be excused, even if it is requested. In a remarkably relevant passage Saint Augustine writes that "it is never licit to kill another: even if he should wish it, indeed if he request it because, hanging between life and death, he begs for help in freeing the soul struggling against the bonds of the body and longing to be released; nor is it licit even when a sick person is no longer able to live." Even when not motivated by a selfish refusal to be burdened with the life of someone who is suffering, euthanasia must be called a *false mercy*, and indeed a disturbing "perversion" of mercy. True "compassion" leads to sharing another's pain; it does not kill the person whose suffering we cannot bear. Moreover, the act of euthanasia appears all the more perverse if it is carried out by those, like relatives, who are supposed to treat a family member with patience and love, or by those, such as doctors, who by virtue of their specific profession are supposed to care for the sick person even in the most painful terminal stages.

The choice of euthanasia becomes more serious when it takes the form of a *murder* committed by others on a person who has in no way requested it and who has never consented to it. The height of arbitrariness and injustice is reached when certain people, such as physicians or legislators, arrogate to themselves the power to decide who ought to live and who ought to die. Once again we find ourselves before the temptation of Eden: to become like God who "knows good and evil." God alone has the power over life and death: "It is I who bring both death and life." But he only exercises this power in accordance with a plan of wisdom and love. When man usurps this power, being enslaved by a foolish and selfish way of thinking, he inevitably uses it for injustice and death. Thus the life of the person who is weak is put into the hands of the one who is strong; in society the sense of justice is lost, and mutual trust, the basis of every authentic interpersonal relationship, is undermined at its root. . . .

All Human Life Has Value

The commandment "You shall not kill," even in its more positive aspects of respecting, loving and promoting human life, is binding on every individual human being. It resounds in the moral conscience of everyone as an irrepressible echo of the original covenant of God the Creator with mankind. It can be recognized by everyone through the light of reason and it can be observed thanks to the mysterious working of the Spirit who, blowing where he wills, comes to and involves every person living in this world.

It is therefore a service of love which we are all committed to ensure to our neighbour, that his or her life may be always defended and promoted, especially when it is weak or threatened. It is not only a personal but a social concern which we must all foster: a concern to make unconditional respect for human life the foundation of a renewed society.

John Paul II, *Evangelium Vitae* (The Gospel of Life), March 25, 1995. www.vatican.va/holy_father/john_paul_ii/encyclicals/john-paul-ii_encyclical_25-march-1995_evangelium-vitae_english.html.

Document 2: Rethinking Life and Death

Peter Singer is a prominent Australian bioethicist whose appointment as the DeCamp professor at Princeton University's Center for Human Values in 1998 caused considerable controversy, in part because of Singer's views about euthanasia. In this excerpt from his book Rethinking Life and Death: The Collapse of Our Traditional Ethics, *Singer argues that the traditional view that all life is sacred needs to be replaced with the idea that quality of life can vary with each individual.*

First Old Commandment:
Treat all human life as of equal worth.

Hardly anyone really believes that all human life is of equal worth. The rhetoric that flow so easily from the pens and mouths of popes, theologians, ethicists, and some doctors is belied every time these same people accept that we need not go all out to save a severely malformed baby; that we may allow an elderly man with advanced Alzheimer's disease to die from pneumonia, untreated by antibiotics; or that we can withdraw food and water from a patient in a persistent vegetative state. . . . The new approach is able to deal with these situations in the obvious way, without struggling to reconcile them with any lofty claims that all human life is of equal worth, irrespective of its potential for gaining or regaining consciousness.

First New Commandment:
Recognize that the worth of human life varies.
  This new commandment allows us frankly to acknowledge . . . that life without consciousness is of no worth at all. We can reach the same view . . . about a life that has no possibility of mental, social, or physical interaction with other human beings. Where life is not one of total or near total deprivation, the new ethic will judge the worth of continued life by taking into account both predictable suffering and possible compensations.
  Consistent with the first new commandment, we should treat human beings in accordance with their ethically relevant characteristics. Some of these are inherent in the nature of the being. They include consciousness, the capacity for physical, social, and mental interaction with other beings, having conscious preferences for continued life, and having enjoyable experiences. Other relevant aspects depend on the relationship of the being to others—having relatives, for example, who will grieve over your death, or being so situated in a group that if you are killed, others will fear for their own lives. All of these things make a difference to the regard and respect we should have for a being.

Peter Singer, *Rethinking Life and Death: The Collapse of Our Traditional Ethics.* New York: St. Martin's, 1995.

Document 3: Assisted Suicide Is a Form of Euthanasia

The International Anti-Euthanasia Task Force is devoted to preventing euthanasia from being legalized. In the following excerpt from its frequently asked questions (FAQ) sheet, the IAETF explains that suicide is an individual act, but that assisted suicide involves helping another to die and therefore is considered a form of killing.

What is euthanasia?

Answer: Formerly called "mercy killing," euthanasia means intentionally *making* someone die, rather than allowing that person to die naturally. Put bluntly, euthanasia means killing in the name of compassion.

What is the difference between euthanasia and assisted suicide?

Answer: In euthanasia, one person does something that directly kills another. For example, a doctor gives a lethal injection to a patient.
  In assisted suicide, a non-suicidal person knowingly and intentionally provides the means or acts in some way to help a suicidal person kill himself or herself. For example, a doctor writes a prescription for poison, or someone hooks up a face mask and tubing to a canister of carbon monoxide and then instructs the suicidal person on how to push a lever so that she'll be gassed to death.

For all practical purposes, any distinction between euthanasia and assisted suicide has been abandoned today. Information contained in these answers to frequently asked questions will use the word "euthanasia" for both euthanasia and assisted suicide. . . .

But shouldn't people have the right to commit suicide?

Answer: People do have the power to commit suicide. Suicide and attempted suicide are not criminalized. Each and every year, in the United States alone, there are more suicides than homicides.

Suicide is a tragic, individual act. Euthanasia is not about a private act. It's about letting one person facilitate the death of another. That is a matter of very public concern since it can lead to tremendous abuse, exploitation and erosion of care for the most vulnerable people among us.

Euthanasia is not about giving rights to the person who dies but, instead, is about changing the law and public policy so that doctors, relatives and others can directly and intentionally end another person's life.

This change would not give rights to the person who is killed, but to the person who does the killing. In other words, euthanasia is not about the right to die. It's about the right to kill.

Isn't "kill" too strong a word for euthanasia?

Answer: No. The word "kill" means "to cause the death of."

In 1989, a group of physicians published a report in the *New England Journal of Medicine* in which they concluded that it would be morally acceptable for doctors to give patients suicide information and a prescription for deadly drugs so they can kill themselves. Dr. Ronald Cranford, one of the authors of the report, publicly acknowledged that this is "the same as killing the patient."

While changes in the law would lead to euthanasia being considered a "medical intervention," the reality would not change—the patient would be killed.

Proponents of euthanasia often use euphemisms like "deliverance," "aid-in-dying" and "gentle landing." If a public policy has to be promoted with euphemisms, that may be because the use of accurate, descriptive language would demonstrate that the policy is misguided.

International Anti-Euthanasia Task Force, "Answers to Frequently Asked Questions," 1998. www.iaetf. org/faq.htm.

Document 4: Euthanasia and Individual Liberty

Ronald Dworkin is a professor of law at New York University and the author of Freedom's Law: The Moral Reading of the American Constitution, *from which the following is excerpted. Dworkin argues that the Constitution protects the right of individuals to make decisions about euthanasia for themselves.*

Many people, particularly those who [believe] that human life is a divine gift, believe that ending it deliberately (except, perhaps, as punishment) is always, at any stage, the most profound insult to life's objective value.

It would be wrong to think, however, that those who are more permissive about abortion and euthanasia are indifferent to the value of life. Rather, they disagree about what respecting that value means. They think that in some circumstances—when a fetus is terribly deformed, for example— abortion shows more respect for life than childbirth would. And they think dying with dignity shows more respect for their own lives—better fits their sense of what is really important in and about human existence—than ending their lives in long agony or senseless sedation.

Our constitution takes no sides in these ancient disputes about life's "meaning." But it does protect people's right to die as well as to live, so far as possible, in the light of their own intensely personal convictions, about "the mystery of human life." It insists that these values are too central to personality, too much at the core of liberty, to allow a majority to decide what everyone must believe. Of course the law must protect people who think it would be appalling to be killed, even if they had only painful months or minutes to live anyway. But the law must also protect those with the opposite conviction: that it would be appalling not to be offered an easier, calmer death with the help of doctors they trust. Making someone die in a way that others approve, but that he believes contradicts his own dignity, is a serious, unjustified, unnecessary form of tyranny.

Quoted in Michael M. Uhlmann, ed., *Last Rites? Assisted Suicide and Euthanasia Debated.* Grand Rapids, MI: William B. Eerdmans, 1998.

Document 5: Dying Patients Need Better Care, Not Euthanasia

Herbert Hendin, executive director of the American Suicide Foundation, argues that patients who request euthanasia or assistance in suicide are really asking for relief from suffering. He believes that the legalization of euthanasia would discourage the medical profession from seeking better ways to relieve suffering through the techniques of palliative and hospice care.

Patients who request euthanasia are usually asking in the strongest way they know for mental and physical relief from suffering. When that request is made to a caring, sensitive, and knowledgeable physician who can address their fear, relieve their suffering, and assure them that he or she will remain with them to the end, most patients no longer want to die and are grateful for the time remaining to them.

Advances in our knowledge of palliative care in the past twenty years make clear that humane care for the terminally ill does not require us to legalize assisted suicide and euthanasia. Study has shown that the more physicians know about palliative care the less apt they are to favor legalizing assisted suicide and euthanasia. Our challenge is to bring that knowledge and that care to all patients who are terminally ill.

Our success in meeting the challenge of providing palliative care for those who are terminally ill will do much to preserve our social humanity.

If we do not provide such care, legalization of assisted suicide and euthanasia will become the simplistic answer to the problems of dying. If legalization prevails, we will lose more lives to suicide (although we will call the deaths by a different name) than can be saved by the efforts of the American Suicide Foundation and those of all the other institutions working to prevent suicide in this country.

The tragedy that will befall depressed suicidal patients will be matched by what will happen to terminally ill people, particularly older poor people. Assisted suicide and euthanasia will become routine ways of dealing with serious and terminal illness just as they have in the Netherlands; those without means will be under particular pressure to accept the euthanasia option. In the process, palliative care will be undercut for everyone.

House Committee on the Judiciary, Subcommittee on the Constitution, *Oversight Hearing: Assisted Suicide in the United States*, 104th Congress, 2nd sess., 29 April 1996. www.house.gov/judiciary/2169.htm.

Document 6: *Final Exit*

In 1991 Hemlock Society founder Derek Humphry published the surprise best-seller Final Exit: The Practicalities of Self-Deliverance and Assisted Suicide for the Dying, *in which he describes techniques for committing relatively painless suicide. The book shocked and offended many people, but its success proved to many observers that Americans were concerned about how they would die. The preface to* Final Exit, *written by fellow right-to-die activist Betty Rollin, is excerpted here.*

The real question is, does a person have a right to depart from life when he or she is nearing the end and has nothing but horror ahead? And, if necessary, should a physician be permitted to help? Because of what I saw my mother go through, and what I know now about the suffering of others, my answer to those questions is yes.

The medical establishment sometimes makes the point that if pain medication were adequately dispensed, people wouldn't want to die. The fine efforts of hospice notwithstanding, that 'if' is one of the biggest I know.

Some people want to eke out every second of life—no matter how grim—and that is their right. But others do not. And that should be **their** right. Until it is, until there is a law which would allow physicians to help people who want a final exit, here is Derek Humphry's book, fittingly named, to guide them.

Derek Humphry, *Final Exit: The Practicalities of Self-Deliverance and Assisted Suicide for the Dying*. Eugene, OR: Hemlock Society, 1991.

Document 7: The Fourteenth Amendment

The parties in the U.S. Supreme Court cases from Washington and New York who argued that patients have a constitutional right to physician-assisted suicide based their arguments in part on the Due Process Clause of the Fourteenth Amendment to the Constitution, reproduced here. The Supreme Court has ruled that this clause, in some cases, protects an individual's right to make his or her own decisions. (This is often referred to as the "liberty interest" of the Fourteenth Amendment.)

No state shall make or enforce any law which shall abridge the privileges or immunities of citizens of the United States; nor shall any state deprive any person of life, liberty, or property, without due process of law; nor deny to any person within its jurisdiction the equal protection of the laws.

Document 8: The Ninth Circuit Recognizes a Constitutional Right to Physician-Assisted Suicide

On March 6, 1996, the Ninth Circuit Court of Appeals released its decision in the case of Compassion in Dying v. Washington, *in which right-to-die activists had argued that Washington State's ban on physician-assisted suicide violated the rights of the terminally ill. Judge Stephen Reinhardt, writing the majority opinion for the court, ruled that a terminally ill patient's right to choose physician-assisted suicide was protected by the liberty interest of the Fourteenth Amendment.*

We hold that a liberty interest exists in the choice of how and when one dies, and that the provision of the Washington statute banning assisted suicide, as applied to competent, terminally ill adults who wish to hasten their deaths by obtaining medication prescribed by their doctors, violates the Due Process Clause. . . .

By permitting the individual to exercise the right to choose we are following the constitutional mandate to take such decisions out of the hands of the government, both state and federal, and to put them where they rightly belong, in the hands of the people. We are allowing individuals to make the decisions that so profoundly affect their very existence—and precluding the state from intruding excessively into that critical realm. The Constitution and the courts stand as a bulwark between individual freedom and arbitrary and intrusive governmental power. Under our constitutional system, neither the state nor the majority of the people in a state can impose its will upon the individual in a matter so highly "central to personal dignity and autonomy." Those who believe strongly that death must come without physician assistance are free to follow that creed, be they doctors or patients. They are not free, however, to force their views, their religious convictions, or their philosophies on all the other members of a democratic society, and to compel those whose values differ with theirs to die painful, protracted, and agonizing deaths.

Compassion in Dying v. Washington, opinion text. www.rights.org/deathnet/us9.html.

Document 9: The Supreme Court Rejects a Constitutional Right to Physician-Assisted Suicide

On June 26, 1997, in the case of Washington v. Glucksberg, *the Supreme Court overturned the decision of the Ninth Circuit Court of Appeals, ruling that termi-*

nally ill patients do not have a constitutionally protected right to physician-assisted suicide. Chief Justice William Rehnquist, writing the majority opinion for the Court, ruled that Washington's ban on assisted suicide was constitutional because it advanced several legitimate state interests, including the preservation of human life.

The history of the law's treatment of assisted suicide in this country has been and continues to be one of the rejection of nearly all efforts to permit it. That being the case, our decisions lead us to conclude that the asserted "right" to assistance in committing suicide is not a fundamental liberty interest protected by the Due Process Clause. The Constitution also requires, however, that Washington's assisted suicide ban be rationally related to legitimate government interests. This requirement is unquestionably met here. Washington's assisted suicide ban implicates a number of state interests.

First, Washington has an "unqualified interest in the preservation of human life." The State's prohibition on assisted suicide, like all homicide laws, both reflects and advances its commitment to this interest. . . .

Relatedly, all admit that suicide is a serious public health problem, especially among persons in otherwise vulnerable groups.

Those who attempt suicide—terminally ill or not—often suffer from depression or other mental disorders. . . . Thus, legal physician assisted suicide could make it more difficult for the State to protect depressed or mentally ill persons, or those who are suffering from untreated pain, from suicidal impulses.

The State also has an interest in protecting the integrity and ethics of the medical profession. In contrast to the Court of Appeals' conclusion that "the integrity of the medical profession would [not] be threatened in any way by [physician assisted suicide]," the American Medical Association, like many other medical and physicians' groups, has concluded that "physician assisted suicide is fundamentally incompatible with the physician's role as healer." And physician assisted suicide could, it is argued, undermine the trust that is essential to the doctor patient relationship by blurring the time honored line between healing and harming.

Next, the State has an interest in protecting vulnerable groups—including the poor, the elderly, and disabled persons—from abuse, neglect, and mistakes. . . . If physician assisted suicide were permitted, many might resort to it to spare their families the substantial financial burden of end of life health care costs.

The State's interest here goes beyond protecting the vulnerable from coercion; it extends to protecting disabled and terminally ill people from prejudice, negative and inaccurate stereotypes, and "societal indifference." The State's assisted suicide ban reflects and reinforces its policy that the lives of terminally ill, disabled, and elderly people must be no less valued than the lives of the young and healthy, and that a seriously disabled person's suicidal impulses should be interpreted and treated the same way as anyone else's.

Finally, the State may fear that permitting assisted suicide will start it down the path to voluntary and perhaps even involuntary euthanasia. . . . It turns out that what is couched as a limited right to "physician assisted suicide" is likely, in effect, a much broader license, which could prove extremely difficult to police and contain. Washington's ban on assisting suicide prevents such erosion. . . .

We need not weigh exactingly the relative strengths of these various interests. They are unquestionably important and legitimate, and Washington's ban on assisted suicide is at least reasonably related to their promotion and protection. We therefore hold that Wash. Rev. Code §9A.36.060(1) (1994) does not violate the Fourteenth Amendment, either on its face or "as applied to competent, terminally ill adults who wish to hasten their deaths by obtaining medication prescribed by their doctors."

Throughout the Nation, Americans are engaged in an earnest and profound debate about the morality, legality, and practicality of physician assisted suicide. Our holding permits this debate to continue, as it should in a democratic society. The decision of the en banc Court of Appeals is reversed, and the case is remanded for further proceedings consistent with this opinion.

Washington v. Glucksberg, opinion text. http://supct.law.cornell.edu/supct/html/96-110.ZO.html.

Document 10: The Oregon Death with Dignity Act

The issue of physician-assisted suicide was put on the ballot in Oregon as "Measure 16," which voters there passed in 1994. The law was held up in the courts for a few years, but finally went into effect in October 1997. Much of the Oregon Death with Dignity Act is devoted to the criteria that patients must meet in order to receive physician assistance in suicide. The final portion that patients and witnesses must sign is excerpted here.

REQUEST FOR MEDICATION
TO END MY LIFE IN A HUMANE AND DIGNIFIED MANNER

I, _____, am an adult of sound mind.

I am suffering from _____, which my attending physician has determined is a terminal disease and which has been medically confirmed by a consulting physician.

I have been fully informed of my diagnosis, prognosis, the nature of medication to be prescribed and potential associated risks, the expected result, and the feasible alternatives, including comfort care, hospice care and pain control.

I request that my attending physician prescribe medication that will end my life in a humane and dignified manner.

INITIAL ONE:

_____ I have informed my family of my decision and taken their opinions into consideration.

_____ I have decided not to inform my family of my decision.

_____ I have no family to inform of my decision.

I understand that I have the right to rescind this request at any time.

I understand the full import of this request and I expect to die when I take the medication to be prescribed.

I make this request voluntarily and without reservation, and I accept full moral responsibility for my actions.

Signed: _____

Dated: _____

DECLARATION OF WITNESSES

We declare that the person signing this request:

(a) Is personally known to us or has provided proof of identity;

(b) Signed this request in our presence;

(c) Appears to be of sound mind and not under duress, fraud or undue influence;

(d) Is not a patient for whom either of us is attending physician.

_____ Witness   1/Date

_____ Witness   2/Date

Document 11: Potential Criteria for Physician-Assisted Suicide

In 1991, Dr. Timothy E. Quill published, in the New England Journal of Medicine, *an account of how he had helped a severely ill patient to die by giving her a bottle of sleeping pills and advising her on how many were necessary to commit suicide. A year later, he coauthored a policy proposal for the legalization of PAS, entitled "Care of the Hopelessly Ill: Potential Clinical Criteria for Physician Assisted Suicide," later reprinted in his book,* Death and Dignity: Making Choices and Taking Charge. *In addition to the criteria mentioned here, Quill believes that patients should receive assistance in suicide from doctors they already know and trust, that multiple doctors should confirm the patient's diagnosis, and that there be clear documentation to prove that each criterion is met.*

Because assisted suicide is extraordinary and irreversible treatment, the patient's primary physician must ensure the conditions set forth below are clearly satisfied before proceeding:

1. *The patient must, of his own free will and at his own initiative, clearly and repeatedly request to die rather than continue suffering.* The physician should have a thorough understanding of what continued life would mean to the patient and on what basis the patient deems death preferable. A physician's too-ready acceptance of a patient's request could be perceived as encouragement to commit suicide, yet we also don't want to be so prohibitive or reticent that the patient is forced to "beg" for assistance. Understanding the patient's desire to die and ensuring that the request is enduring are critical in evaluating the patient's rationality, and in assuring that all alternative means of relieving suffering have been adequately

explored. Any sign of patient ambivalence or uncertainty should abort the process, as a clear, convincing, and continuous desire for an end of suffering through death is a strict requirement to proceed. Requests for assisted suicide by advance directive or by a health care surrogate should not be honored.

2. *The patient's judgment must not be distorted.* The patient must be capable of understanding the decision and its implications and consequences. The presence of depression is relevant if it is distorting rational decision making and is reversible in a way that would substantially alter the situation. Expert psychiatric evaluation should be sought when the primary physician is inexperienced in the diagnosis and treatment of depression, or when there is any uncertainty about the rationality of the request or the presence of a reversible mental disorder that would substantially change the patient's perception of his condition once treated.

3. *The patient must have a condition that is incurable, and associated with severe, unrelenting, intolerable suffering.* The patient must understand his condition, prognosis, and the comfort care alternatives available. Though we anticipate that most patients making this request will be imminently terminal, we acknowledge the inexactness of such prognostications, and do not want to arbitrarily exclude persons with incurable, but not imminently terminal, progressive illnesses such as ALS or multiple sclerosis. When there is considerable uncertainty about the patient's medical condition or prognosis, second opinions should be sought and the uncertainty clarified as much as possible before a final response to the patient's request is made.

4. *The physician must ensure that the patient's suffering and the request are not the result of inadequate comfort care.* All reasonable comfort-oriented measures must have been at least considered, and preferably tried, before providing the means for a physician-assisted suicide. Physician-assisted suicide must never be used to circumvent the struggle to provide comprehensive comfort care, or find acceptable alternatives. The physician's willingness to provide assisted suicide in the future is legitimate and important to discuss if raised by the patient, since many will probably find the potential of an escape more important than the reality.

Timothy E. Quill, *Death and Dignity: Making Choices and Taking Charge.* New York: W.W. Norton, 1993. ·

Document 12: A Change of Heart on Assisted Suicide

Diane E. Meier is a professor of geriatrics and director of the Palliative Care Initiative at the Mount Sinai School of Medicine in New York City. In 1992 she, and Timothy Quill, coauthored the proposal to legalize physician-assisted suicide that is excerpted in Document 11. However, in 1998 she wrote the following New York Times *article, "A Change of Heart on Assisted Suicide," in which she expressed her doubts about whether the guidelines she and Quill had proposed could be realistically implemented.*

Some years ago, I believed that doctor-assisted suicide should be legalized and that terminally ill people in great pain deserved more control over the circumstances of their death.

It is true that terminally ill patients sometimes find themselves in truly unbearable circumstances. But after caring for many patients myself, I now think that the risks of assisted suicide outweigh the benefits.

Proponents of doctor-assisted suicide say that strict regulations can reduce the chances of abuse and protect the most vulnerable from feeling coerced. But rules would be difficult, if not impossible, to enforce. For instance, Oregon, the only state to legalize assisted suicide, has guidelines that mandate the following:

A patient must be mentally alert. It is the rare dying patient, particularly if elderly, who remains consistently capable of rational deliberation about medical alternatives. Intermittent confusion, anxiety and depression are the rule rather than the exception, inevitably clouding judgment.

A patient must be within six months of death. Abundant evidence shows that accurately predicting when patients are going to die doesn't become possible until just days before death. The guidelines assume that such a prognosis is possible and deny the uncertainty inherent in such predictions.

A doctor must certify that the patient's decision is not coerced. This is an impossible task, given the financial and other burdens that seriously ill patients pose to their families. Indeed, legalizing assisted suicide is coercive in and of itself. Society would no longer promote the value of each life, and instead sanction an expedient death rather than continued care and support.

The push to legalize doctor-assisted suicide could not come at a worse time. Spiraling health costs and our aging population have led to radical changes in how care is financed, with doctors and hospitals rewarded for doing less for their patients. Seriously ill people need help easing their pain, time to talk to their doctor, answers to their questions and reasonable attempts to prolong their life when death is not imminent.

If this kind of care were available to every patient, it would certainly reduce, if not eliminate, the desire for hastened death. But legalizing assisted suicide would become a cheap and easy way to avoid the costly and time intensive care needed by the terminally ill. It could be seen as an appealing alternative when resources are stretched and family members and doctors are exhausted. The terminally ill patient could feel subtle and not so subtle pressure to opt for suicide. Our society should not be reduced to offering patients a choice between inadequate care and suicide.

The proposed guidelines for assisted suicide are well-meaning, but unrealistic and largely irrelevant to the reality faced by the dying. While I have had patients whose desire to die was compelling and understandable, such patients are few. The distress of the last days, when it occurs, can be effectively treated with analgesic and sedatives. Although we have the knowledge and tools to reduce suffering near the end of life, we are debating instead whether it should be legal for doctors to hasten death.

Diane E. Meier, "A Change of Heart on Assisted Suicide," *New York Times*, April 24, 1998.

Document 13: Assisted Suicide: A Disability Perspective

Much of the opposition to physician-assisted suicide comes from people with disabilities, who fear that they will be pressured by doctors and society to choose assisted death if it becomes a legal option. In 1997 the National Council on Disability, an independent agency within the federal government that acts as a voice for Americans with disabilities, issued a position paper on physician-assisted suicide, which is excerpted below.

The benefits of permitting physician-assisted suicide are substantial and should not be discounted; they include respect for individual autonomy, liberty, and the right to make one's own choices about matters concerning one's intimate personal welfare; affording the dignity of control and choice for a patient who otherwise has little control of her or his situation; allowing the patient to select the time and circumstances of death rather than being totally at the mercy of the terminal medical condition; safeguarding the doctor/patient relationship in making this final medical decision; giving the patient the option of dying in an alert condition rather than in a medicated haze during the last hours of life; and, most importantly, giving the patient the ability to avoid severe pain and suffering.

More Harm Than Good

The Council finds, however, that at the present time such considerations are outweighed by other weighty countervailing realities. The benefits of physician-assisted suicide only apply to the small number of people who actually have an imminently terminal condition, are in severe, untreatable pain, wish to commit suicide, and are unable to do so without a doctor's involvement.

The dangers of permitting physician-assisted suicide are immense. The pressures upon people with disabilities to choose to end their lives, and the insidious appropriation by others of the right to make that choice for them are already prevalent and will continue to increase as managed health care and limitations upon health care resources precipitate increased "rationing" of health care services and health care financing.

People with disabilities are among society's most likely candidates for ending their lives, as society has frequently made it clear that it believes they would be better off dead, or better that they had not been born. The experience in the Netherlands demonstrates that legalizing assisted suicide generates strong pressures upon individuals and families to utilize that option, and leads very quickly to coercion and involuntary euthanasia. If assisted suicide were to become legal, the lives of people with any disability deemed too difficult to live with would be at risk, and persons with disabilities who are poor or members of racial minorities would likely be in the most jeopardy of all.

If assisted suicide were to be legalized, the only way to ward off the most dire ramifications for people with disabilities would be to create stringent procedural prerequisites. But, to be effective, such procedural safeguards would necessarily sacrifice individual autonomy to the supervision of medical and legal overlords to an unacceptable degree—the cure being as bad as the disease.

Help the Disabled to Improve Their Lives, Not to Die

For many people with disabilities, it is more often the discrimination, prejudice, and barriers that they encounter, and the restrictions and lack of options that this society has imposed, rather than their disabilities or their physical pain, that cause people with disabilities' lives to be unsatisfactory and painful. The notion that a decision to choose assisted suicide must be preceded by a full explanation of the programs, resources, and options available to assist the patient if he or she does not decide to pursue suicide strikes *many* people with disabilities as a very shallow promise when they know that all too often the programs are too few, the resources are too limited, and the options are nonexistent. Society should not be ready to give up on the lives of its citizens with disabilities until it has made real and persistent efforts to give these citizens a fair and equal chance to achieve a meaningful life.

For these reasons, the Council has decided that at this time in the history of American society it opposes the legalization of assisted suicide. Current evidence indicates clearly that the interests of the few people who would benefit from legalizing physician-assisted suicide are heavily outweighed by the probability that any law, procedures, and standards that can be imposed to regulate physician-assisted suicide will be misapplied to unnecessarily end the lives of people with disabilities and entail an intolerable degree of intervention by legal and medical officials in such decisions. On balance, the current illegality of physician-assisted suicide is preferable to the limited benefits to be gained by its legalization. At least until such time as our society provides a comprehensive, fully-funded, and operational system of assistive living services for people with disabilities, this is the only position that the National Council on Disability can, in good conscience, support.

National Council on Disability, "Assisted Suicide: A Disability Perspective," March 24, 1997. www.ncd.gov/publications/suicide.html.

Document 14: The Financial Argument for Legalizing Physician-Assisted Suicide

Opponents of euthanasia often claim that if it is legalized, people will be pressured into choosing a hastened death because of financial concerns. End-of-life care can be expensive, so whoever is paying for such treatment—whether it is family members, a private insurance company, or the government—could often save money if terminally ill patients chose to hasten their deaths. In Freedom to Die: People, Politics, and the Right-to-Die Movement, *Derek Humphry and Mary Clement address this concern, contending that the high cost of end-of-life care also provides a good argument* for *the legalization of assisted suicide.*

A rational argument can be made for allowing PAS in order to offset the amount society and family spend on the ill, *as long as it is the voluntary wish* of the mentally competent terminally and incurably ill adult. There will likely come a time when PAS becomes a commonplace occurrence for individuals who *want* to die and feel it is the right thing to do by their loved ones. There is no contradicting the fact that since the largest medical expenses are incurred in the final days and weeks of life, the hastened demise of people with only a short time left would free resources for others. Hundreds of billions of dollars could benefit those patients who not only *can* be cured but who also *want* to live. What possible sense does it make to use limited resources on people who *cannot* be helped and who *do not want* to be helped, either because they themselves have had "enough" or because they believe it is the morally correct thing to do for their family?

It is this kind of thinking that concerns critics of an assisted death. Opponents of the practice are repelled by the thought of assisted suicide as an answer to shrinking health care resources. Supporters of the practice respond that no one is forcing, coercing, or encouraging anyone to do anything. Assisted death is totally *voluntary*—a matter to be decided with the family and with the patient's conscience. The debate goes round and round, and few, if any, change their minds. . . .

The American public is uncomfortable talking about the money connection, focusing instead on the right of the patient to a dignified death. Herein lies the unspoken argument for physician aid in dying. The rising cost of health care is a societal reality that has promoted a rush of populist interest in constructing a new culture of dying in the United States, focusing on shortening the dying process for those who want it. It is the unspoken connection of value to cost—for the nation, business, and the family unit. In advocating for an assisted death, one is beginning to hear the argument that says: "Look, let's face facts. The nation's economy is about to break under the growing cost of health care and the situation will get markedly worse as baby boomers become elderly and infirmed patients eating at the subsidized table. Families are suffering. Even if reform takes place, how comprehensive will it be? Politicians know it's a losing issue at the ballot box. If someone wants to bail out a little early, why should we stop them? Let's put our energies toward guidelines that will enable the practice to go as smoothly as possible. We certainly won't encourage people to hasten their death, but why should we stop them? Physician-assisted suicide is a win-win situation." Spend some time on the subject, and this unspoken argument will surface—on an ever more frequent basis. It is a pragmatic argument and one that deserves an answer.

Derek Humphry and Mary Clement, *Freedom to Die: People, Politics, and the Right-to-Die Movement.* New York: St. Martin's, 1998.

Document 15: Involuntary Euthanasia in the Netherlands

Since the 1970s, doctors in the Netherlands have not been prosecuted for per-forming euthanasia if they follow certain guidelines, the most important of which is that the patient specifically requests it. However, in 1990, the Dutch govern-ment commissioned a study of euthanasia which revealed that many doctors has-tened the death of patients without their explicit consent. The Remmelink report, as it is called, stated that about 1,000 deaths per year were from "termination of life without the patient's explicit request." Wesley J. Smith, author of Forced Exit: The Slippery Slope from Assisted Suicide to Legalized Murder, *be-lieves that the actual number of cases of involuntary euthanasia is even higher if one counts the doctors who used large amounts of pain medication to hasten death.*

It is important to recall that when euthanasia was first accepted in the Netherlands, it was supposed to be a rare event, to be resorted to only in the most unusual cases of "intolerable suffering." The guidelines were designed specifically to keep euthanasia occurrences few and far between by establishing demanding conditions that must be met. Over time, however, doctors began to interpret the conditions loosely and even ignore them.

This is the typical pattern of the euthanasia movement. Killing by doc-tors is always presented to the public as a "rare" occurrence, to be applied only when nothing else can be done. Proponents soothingly assure a doubtful public, as the New York euthanasia advocate Dr. Timothy Quill puts it, that euthanasia will be restricted to "the patient of last resort, [to be] taken only when hospice care stops providing comfort and dignity," when "all alternatives have been exhausted." (Hospice medical care is designed to help terminally ill people. It does not seek to cure the termi-nal illness. Rather, it provides comfort, care, and alleviation of symptoms for dying people.) Unfortunately, the Dutch experience clearly demon-strates that once killing is accepted as a legitimate medical act, it quickly ceases to be rare or is resorted to only when all else fails. . . .

In 1990, responding to the heated debate about Dutch euthanasia and the many anecdotes being told about involuntary killings of patients by doctors, the Dutch government decided to determine how euthanasia was actually being carried out and appointed an investigative committee. Called the Committee to Investigate the Medical Practice Concerning Euthanasia, it was commonly known as the Remmelink Commission, after the committee's chairman, Professor J. Remmelink, then the attorney gen-eral of the Dutch Supreme Court. . . .

According to the Remmelink Report, about 130,000 people die each year in the Netherlands. Of these, approximately 43,300, or about one third, die suddenly—from catastrophic heart attacks, stroke, accidents, et cetera—thus precluding medical decision making about end-of-life care. That leaves approximately 90,000 people whose deaths involve end-of-life medical decision making each year. With that in mind, here are the figures about euthanasia-related deaths in 1990, derived from the Remmelink Report's published statistical data:

- 2,300 patients were euthanized (killed) by their doctors upon request, and 400 people died through physician-assisted suicide, for a total of 2,700 doctor-induced deaths. That is approximately 3 percent of all deaths involving end-of-life medical care. The equivalent percentage in the United States would be 41,500 deaths.

- 1,040 died from involuntary euthanasia, lethal injections given without request or consent—three deaths every single day. These deaths constitute slightly more than 1 percent of all cases involving end-of-life medical care. (The same percentage in the United States would be approximately 16,000 involuntary killings per year.) Of these involuntary euthanasia cases, 14 percent, or 145, were fully competent to make their own medical decisions but were killed without request or consent anyway. (The same percentage in the United States would be more than 2,000 who would be killed.) Moreover, 72 percent of the people killed without their consent had never given any indication they would want their lives terminated.

- 8,100 patients died from an intentional overdose of morphine or other pain-control medications, designed primarily to terminate life. In other words, death was not a side effect of treatment to relieve pain, which can sometimes occur, but was the *intended result* of the overdose. Of these, 61 percent (4,941 patients) were intentionally overdosed without request or consent. The equivalent percentage in the United States would be approximately 78,000.

These figures are startling. Of the approximately 90,000 Dutch people whose deaths involved end-of-life medical decision making, 11,140 were intentionally killed (euthanized) or assisted in suicide—or 11.1 percent of all Dutch deaths involving medical decision making. This is approximately 8.5 percent of Dutch deaths from all causes. Of these killings, *more than half were involuntary* (1,040 involuntary lethal injections and 4,941 involuntary intentional overdoses). Applying those percentages to the U.S. death rate would mean more than 170,000 deaths each year caused by euthanasia or assisted suicide, and about 85,000 of these involuntary, more than the current number of U.S. suicides and homicides combined.

Wesley J. Smith, *Forced Exit: The Slippery Slope from Assisted Suicide to Legalized Murder.* New York: Times Books, 1997.

Document 16: A Dutch Doctor Defends Euthanasia in the Netherlands

Many opponents of euthanasia have condemned the Netherlands for permitting both physician-assisted suicide and active, voluntary euthanasia. The Remmelink report, which revealed that approximately 1,000 people in the Netherlands per year are victims of involuntary euthanasia, served to fuel this criticism. However, many Dutch, especially Dutch physicians, believe their country's policy is a good one despite the upsetting findings of the Remmelink report. Pieter V. Admiraal, a Dutch anesthesiologist who works with cancer patients, explains this view.

Active euthanasia has been practiced in The Netherlands for more than twenty years. Today the total number of patients is estimated as 3,500 to 4,000 cases a year. Of this number, more than 80% have cancer, meaning that about 9% of our cancer patients will have euthanasia. The remaining group is about equally divided among AIDS patients; patients with multiple sclerosis, amyotrophic lateral sclerosis, and muscular dystrophia; and a group of very old patients with several complaints.

The Dutch position has compassionate supporters and vehement opponents all over the world. Some of these are well informed, while others have gathered their information through hearsay or tendentious articles by opponents. Opponents raise three main problems in accepting euthanasia: the slippery slope argument; the potential for abuse; and the effect on the relationship between patient and doctor.

In my view, after so many years, there is no evidence to support the slippery slope argument. Some will mention that the investigation of [Paul J.] van der Maas has shown that, in about 1,000 cases, 0.8% of all deaths in The Netherlands, life was terminated without the explicit request of the patient. Many articles followed. It became clear that in 60% of these cases the doctor had earlier information about the patient's wishes, albeit short of a specific request; in all other cases the patient was suffering but discussion was not possible.

For me, it is acceptable that a doctor who sees that his long-time patient is suffering and will die within a short time but is unable to express his or her wishes may consider it a duty to shorten the patient's life. But in all these cases a decision has to be made together with the relatives and other care-givers.

Pieter V. Admiraal, "Euthanasia in The Netherlands," *Free Inquiry*, Winter 1996/97.

Document 17: The Hippocratic Oath

The writings of Hippocrates, a Greek physician who lived during the fifth century B.C., have had a great impact on later generations of physicians. Many doctors today still take the Hippocratic oath upon graduation from medical school. Some physicians believe that they should follow the oath's proscription against assisting a patient to commit suicide, while others believe that only the spirit of the oath is important, and that doctors should participate in euthanasia if they feel it is in the best interests of a patient.

I swear by Apollo Physician and Asclepius and Hygieia and Panaceia and all the gods and goddesses, making them my witnesses, that I will fulfill according to my ability and judgment this oath and this covenant:

To hold him who has taught me this art as equal to my parents and to live my life in partnership with him, and if he is in need of money to give him a share of mine, and to regard his offspring as equal to my brothers in male lineage and to teach them this art—if they desire to learn it—without fee and covenant; to give a share of precepts and oral instruction and all the other learning to my sons and to the sons of him who has instructed me and to pupils who have signed the covenant and have taken an oath according to the medical law, but to no one else.

I will apply dietetic measures for the benefit of the sick according to my ability and judgment; I will keep them from harm and injustice.

I will neither give a deadly drug to anybody if asked for it, nor will I make a suggestion to this effect. Similarly I will not give to a woman an abortive remedy. In purity and holiness I will guard my life and my art.

I will not use the knife, not even on sufferers from stone, but will withdraw in favor of such men as are engaged in this work.

Whatever houses I may visit, I will come for the benefit of the sick, remaining free of all intentional injustice, of all mischief and in particular of sexual relations with both female and male persons, be they free or slaves.

What I may see or hear in the course of the treatment or even outside of the treatment in regard to the life of men, which on no account one must spread abroad, I will keep to myself holding such things shameful to be spoken about.

If I fulfill this oath and do not violate it, may it be granted to me to enjoy life and art, being honored with fame among all men for all time to come; if I transgress it and swear falsely, may the opposite of all this be my lot.

Document 18: Physician-Assisted Suicide Violates Medical Ethics

The American Medical Association has long been opposed to the legalization of physician-assisted suicide, pledging instead to step up efforts to train doctors in pain management and to meet other needs of dying patients. This excerpt from the AMA's Code of Medical Ethics *sums up its position.*

Physician assisted suicide occurs when a physician facilitates a patient's death by providing the necessary means and/or information to enable the patient to perform the life-ending act (e.g., the physician provides sleeping pills and information about the lethal dose, while aware that the patient may commit suicide).

It is understandable, though tragic, that some patients in extreme duress—such as those suffering from a terminal, painful, debilitating illness—may come to decide that death is preferable to life. However, allowing physicians to participate in assisted suicide would cause more harm than good. Physician assisted suicide is fundamentally incompatible with the physician's role as healer, would be difficult or impossible to control, and would pose serious societal risks.

Instead of participating in assisted suicide, physicians must aggressively respond to the needs of patients at the end of life. Patients should not be abandoned once it is determined that cure is impossible. Patients near the end of life must continue to receive emotional support, comfort care, adequate pain control, respect for patient autonomy, and good communication.

Quoted in Michael M. Uhlmann, ed., *Last Rights? Assisted Suicide and Euthanasia Debated.* Grand Rapids, MI: William B. Eerdmans, 1998.

Document 19: Physician-Assisted Suicide Does Not Violate Medical Ethics

In his book Final Acts of Love: Families, Friends, and Assisted Dying, *Stephen Jamison includes a section in which he answers frequently asked questions regarding physician-assisted suicide. In this excerpt, he sums up why supporters of assisted suicide believe it is compatible with medical ethics.*

How is assisted death compatible with biomedical ethics?
The four principles of biomedical ethics include beneficence, nonmaleficence, autonomy, and justice. Beneficence can be understood as the opportunity for a patient to be released from suffering. Nonmaleficence, to do no harm, can be interpreted as doing less harm by not prolonging unnecessary suffering. Autonomy can be seen by respecting the rights, desires, individuality, and personhood of the patient, with final authority for all decisions resting with this person. And justice can reside in equality of care for all terminally ill with availability for both hospice care and aid-in-dying.

Stephen Jamison, *Final Acts of Love: Families, Friends, and Assisted Dying.* New York: G.P. Putnam's Sons, 1995.

Document 20: It's Over, Debbie

The Journal of the American Medical Association *published this anonymous article in 1988. Although it is not even clear whether the euthanasia incident it describes actually occurred, the piece stimulated vigorous debate within the medical community over the ethics of active, voluntary euthanasia.*

The call came in the middle of the night. As a gynecology resident rotating through a large, private hospital, I had come to detest telephone calls, because invariably I would be up for several hours and would not feel good the next day. However, duty called, so I answered the phone. A nurse informed me that a patient was having difficulty getting rest, could I please see her. She was on 3 North. That was the gynecologic-oncology unit, not my usual duty station. As I trudged along, bumping sleepily against walls and corners and not believing I was up again, I tried to imagine what I might find at the end of my walk. Maybe an elderly woman with an anxiety reaction, or perhaps something particularly horrible.

I grabbed the chart from the nurses station on my way to the patient's room, and the nurse gave me some hurried details: a 20-year-old girl named Debbie was dying of ovarian cancer. She was having unrelenting vomiting apparently as the result of an alcohol drip administered for sedation. Hmmm, I thought. Very sad. As I approached the room I could hear loud, labored breathing. I entered and saw an emaciated, dark-haired woman who appeared much older than 20. She was receiving nasal oxygen, had an IV, and was sitting in bed suffering from what was obviously severe air hunger. The chart noted her weight at 80 pounds. A second woman, also dark-haired but of middle age, stood at her right, holding her hand. Both looked up as I entered. The room seemed filled with the patient's desperate effort to survive. Her eyes were hollow, and she had suprasternal and intercostal retractions with her rapid inspirations. She had not eaten or slept in two days. She had not responded to chemotherapy and was being given supportive care only. It was a gallows scene, a cruel mockery of her youth and unfulfilled potential. Her only words to me were, "Let's get this over with."

I retreated with my thoughts to the nurses station. The patient was tired and needed rest. I could not give her health, but I could give her rest. I asked the nurse to draw 20 mg of morphine sulfate into a syringe. Enough, I thought, to do the job. I took the syringe into the room and told the two women I was going to give Debbie something that would let her rest and to say good-bye. Debbie looked at the syringe, then laid her head on the pillow with her eyes open, watching what was left of the world. I injected the morphine intravenously and watched to see if my calculations on its effects would be correct. Within seconds her breathing slowed to a normal rate, her eyes closed, and her features softened as she seemed restful at last. The older woman stroked the hair of the now-sleeping patient. I waited for the inevitable next effect of depressing the respiratory drive. With clocklike certainty, within four minutes the breathing rate slowed even more, then became irregular, then ceased. The dark-haired woman stood erect and seemed relieved.

It's over, Debbie.

Anonymous, "It's Over, Debbie," *Journal of the American Medical Association*, January 8, 1998.

STUDY QUESTIONS

Chapter 1

1. According to Viewpoint 1, what are the three main criteria for justifiable euthanasia?

2. Viewpoint 1 contends that euthanasia is sometimes the most compassionate way to relieve a dying person's suffering. How does Viewpoint 2 respond to this argument? Do you believe that euthanasia is an acceptable way to relieve suffering?

3. According to Viewpoint 2, the killing of an innocent human being is always wrong. How does Viewpoint 1 address the idea that euthanasia is killing, and the claim that all human life is sacred? Which position do you agree with, and why?

4. Explain the difference between active and passive euthanasia. Do you agree with Viewpoint 3's claim that letting a person die is morally equivalent to killing him or her? Why does George Annas in Viewpoint 4 believe that this argument is "patently absurd"?

5. According to Viewpoint 3, why is active euthanasia sometimes preferable to passive euthanasia?

6. According to Viewpoint 4, why is passive euthanasia legal? What does the New York State Task Force on Life and Law say would happen if passive euthanasia were still illegal? In contrast, what single reason does Viewpoint 3 offer as justification for passive euthanasia? Which explanation do you think is closer to the truth? Explain your answer.

7. Explain the doctrine of double effect, as described in Viewpoint 4. According to this doctrine, when a physician causes the death of a patient, what determines whether or not the physician has acted properly?

Chapter 2

1. What does the Hippocratic oath say regarding physician-assisted suicide? How do Viewpoint 1 and Viewpoint 2 each describe the Hippocratic oath's importance to doctors today?

2. Part of the debate over physician-assisted suicide involves society's conflicting views over what the role of physicians

should be. In Viewpoint 2, what does Marcia Angell claim is the "highest ethical imperative of doctors"? How does this contrast with the American Medical Association's description of a doctor's pledge in Viewpoint 2?

3. One summary of a physician's duties, emphasized in Viewpoint 2, is that doctors should do whatever is in the best interests of their patients. But according to Viewpoint 1, there is no objective way for doctors to decide when death would benefit a patient and when it would not. Do you find this argument convincing? Why or why not?

Chapter 3

1. Viewpoint 1 argues that individuals have the right to control their own deaths, while in Viewpoint 2 Hadley V. Arkes argues that individuals do not have the right to kill themselves. Which argument do you find most persuasive, and why?

2. Viewpoint 1 contends that laws against physician-assisted suicide and euthanasia are unjust because they violate an individual's right to privacy, and because they may be influenced by religious beliefs. Do you believe that euthanasia is strictly an individual choice, or do you agree with Viewpoint 2 that society and the government have a right to regulate these practices? Defend your answer.

3. In Viewpoint 3, M. Scott Peck argues that the government should recognize a patient's right to hospice care before it recognizes a right to physician-assisted suicide. Based on their statements in Viewpoint 4, do you think Timothy E. Quill and the Hemlock Society would disagree with this claim? Provide reasons for your answer.

4. Viewpoint 3 argues that if assisted suicide becomes legal, depressed and suicidal persons will be more likely to utilize the option, and other dying patients will be pressured into choosing an early death. How does Barbara Dority address this concern in Viewpoint 4? Which view do you agree with, and why?

5. Viewpoint 5 links the debate over euthanasia to the American experience with abortion. Do you think it is appropriate to compare the two controversies? Why or why not?

6. Viewpoint 5 cites reports from the Netherlands which reveal that some doctors there have ignored Dutch euthanasia guidelines. How does Viewpoint 6 defend these incidents? Do you think the abuses of euthanasia in the Netherlands lend credence to the slippery slope theory? Explain your answer.

Organizations to Contact

The editors have compiled the following list of organizations concerned with the issues debated in this book. The descriptions are derived from materials provided by the organizations. All have publications or information available for interested readers. The list was compiled on the date of publication of the present volume; the information provided here may change. Be aware that many organizations take several weeks or longer to respond to inquiries, so allow as much time as possible.

American Civil Liberties Union (ACLU)
132 W. 43rd St., New York, NY 10036
(212) 994-9800
website: http://www.aclu.org

The ACLU champions the rights of individuals in right-to-die and euthanasia cases as well as in many other civil rights issues. The Foundation of the ACLU provides legal defense, research, and education. The organization publishes the quarterly *Civil Liberties* and various pamphlets, books, and position papers.

American Life League
PO Box 1350, Stafford, VA 22555
(540) 659-4171 • fax: (540) 659-2586
website: http://www.all.org

The league believes that human life is sacred. It works to educate Americans about the dangers of all forms of euthanasia and opposes legislative efforts that would legalize or increase its incidence. It publishes the bimonthly pro-life magazine *Celebrate Life*, and distributes videos, brochures, and newsletters monitoring euthanasia-related developments.

American Society of Law, Medicine, and Ethics
765 Commonwealth Ave., Suite 1634, Boston, MA 02215
(617) 262-4990 • fax: (617) 437-7596
e-mail: aslme@bu.edu • website: http://www.aslme.org

The society's members include physicians, attorneys, health care administrators, and others interested in the relationship between law, medicine, and ethics. The organization has an information clearinghouse and a library, and it acts as a forum for discussion of issues such as euthanasia and assisted suicide. It publishes the quarterlies *American Journal of Law and Medicine* and *Journal of Law, Medicine, and Ethics*, the newsletter *ASLME Briefings*, and books such as *Legal and Ethical Aspects of Treating Critically and Terminally Ill Patients*.

Choice in Dying (CID)

1035 30th St. NW, Washington, DC 20007
(800) 989-WILL
e-mail: cid@choices.org • website: http://www.choices.org

Choice in Dying is a national, not-for-profit organization dedicated to fostering communication about complex end-of-life decisions among individuals, their loved ones, and health care professionals. The organization invented living wills in 1967 and provides the only national hotline to respond to families and patients during end-of-life crises. CID also provides educational materials, public and professional education, and ongoing monitoring of changes in state and federal right-to-die legislation.

Compassion in Dying Federation

6312 SW Capitol Hwy., Suite 415, Portland, OR 97201
(503) 221-9556 • fax: (503) 228-9610
e-mail: info@compassionindying.org
website: http://www.compassionindying.org

The mission of Compassion in Dying Federation is to provide national leadership for client service, legal advocacy, and public education to improve pain and symptom management, increase patient empowerment and self-determination, and expand end-of-life choices to include aid-in-dying for terminally ill, mentally competent adults.

Euthanasia Prevention Coalition BC

103-2609 Westview Dr., Suite 126
North Vancouver, BC V7N 4N2, CANADA
(604) 795-3772 • fax: (604) 794-3960
website: http://www.epc.bc.ca/

The Euthanasia Prevention Coalition opposes the promotion or legalization of euthanasia and assisted suicide. The coalition's purpose is to educate the public on risks associated with the promotion of euthanasia, increase public awareness of alternative methods for the relief of suffering, and to represent the vulnerable as an advocate before the courts on issues of euthanasia and related subjects. Press releases from the coalition are available at its website.

The Hemlock Society
PO Box 101810, Denver, CO 80250
(800) 247-7421 • (303) 639-1202 • fax: (303) 639-1224
e-mail: hemlock@privatei.com • website:
http://www.hemlock.org/hemlock

The society believes that terminally ill individuals have the right to commit suicide. The society publishes books on suicide, death, and dying, including *Final Exit*, a guide for those suffering with terminal illnesses and considering suicide. The Hemlock Society also publishes the newsletter *TimeLines*.

Human Life International
4 Family Life Ln., Front Royal, VA 22630
(540) 635-7884 • fax: (540) 635-7363
e-mail: hli@hli.org • website: http://www.hli.org

HLI categorically rejects euthanasia and believes assisted suicide is morally unacceptable. It defends the rights of the unborn, the disabled, and those threatened by euthanasia, and it provides education, advocacy, and support services. HLI publishes the monthly newsletters *HLI Reports*, *HLI Update*, and *Deacons Circle*, as well as on-line articles on euthanasia.

International Anti-Euthanasia Task Force (IAETF)
PO Box 760, Steubenville, OH 43952
(740) 282-3810
e-mail: info@iaetf.org • website: http://www.iaetf.org

The task force opposes euthanasia, assisted suicide, and policies that threaten the lives of the medically vulnerable. IAETF publishes fact sheets and position papers on euthanasia-related topics in addition to the bimonthly newsletter, *IAETF Update*. It analyzes the policies and legislation concerning medical and social work organizations and files amicus curiae briefs in major "right-to-die" cases.

National Hospice Organization
1901 N. Moore St., Suite 901, Arlington, VA 22209
(703) 243-5900 • (800) 658-8898 • fax: (703) 525-5762
e-mail: drsnho@cais.org • website: http://www.nho.org

The organization works to educate the public about the benefits of hospice care for the terminally ill and their families. It seeks to promote the idea that with the proper care and pain medication, the terminally ill can live out their lives comfortably and in the company of their families. The organization opposes euthanasia and assisted suicide. It conducts educational and training programs for administrators and caregivers in numerous aspects of hospice care. It publishes the quarterlies *Hospice Journal* and *Hospice Magazine,* as well as books and monographs.

FOR FURTHER READING

Books

Margaret P. Battin, *The Death Debate: Ethical Issues in Suicide.* Upper Saddle River, NJ: Prentice Hall, 1996. The author explores both historical and modern arguments concerning suicide and euthanasia, concentrating on the ethical, religious, and philosophical aspects of the debate.

John Keown, ed., *Euthanasia Examined: Ethical, Clinical and Legal Perspectives.* New York: Cambridge University Press, 1995. This is a good collection of essays in which experts on the topic argue for or against euthanasia.

Edward J. Larson and Darrel W. Amundsen, *A Different Death: Euthanasia in the Christian Tradition.* Downers Grove, IL: Intervarsity, 1998. The authors trace the history of suicide and euthanasia from early Christianity to the modern period. In the last part of the book, the authors provide information on how to approach the euthanasia debate from a Christian perspective.

Michael Manning, *Euthanasia and Physician-Assisted Suicide: Killing or Caring?* Mahwah, NJ: Paulist, 1998. This book provides a good introductory overview of the euthanasia debate. The author, a Roman Catholic priest, devotes considerable time to the church's position on the subject, but other arguments are explored in a relatively evenhanded manner.

Jonathan D. Moreno, ed., *Arguing Euthanasia: The Controversy over Mercy Killing.* New York: Simon & Schuster, 1995. In this excellent collection of viewpoints, authoritative authors address the major arguments for and against euthanasia. Moreno provides a concise overview of the right-to-die movement in the book's introduction.

Lonny Shavelson, *A Chosen Death: The Dying Confront Assisted Suicide.* Berkeley and Los Angeles: University of California Press, 1998. Dr. Shavelson recounts many of the deaths that he has assisted in, explaining why he feels euthanasia was ethical in each case. The book is notable for the perspective it provides on the reasons why many terminally ill people request euthanasia.

Wesley J. Smith, *Forced Exit: The Slippery Slope from Assisted Suicide to Legalized Murder.* New York: Times Books, 1997. Smith, a strong opponent of euthanasia, argues that if legalized, euthanasia will lead to involuntary killing of the terminally ill, the elderly, the disabled, and others. He also provides rebuttals to the major arguments for euthanasia.

Internet Sources

New York State Task Force on Life and the Law, *When Death Is Sought: Assisted Suicide and Euthanasia in the Medical Context.* New York State Department of Health, 1994. www.health.state.ny.us/ nysdoh/provider/death.htm. This comprehensive report provides a detailed analysis of the ethical, medical, and legal issues surrounding the euthanasia debate, and many valuable resources are referenced in footnotes. The task force's final conclusion is that physician-assisted suicide should remain illegal, but the authors are careful to objectively consider every point of view.

WORKS CONSULTED

Books

Donald W. Cox, *Hemlock's Cup: The Struggle for Death with Dignity.* Amherst, NY: Prometheus Books, 1993. Although the author supports euthanasia, this overview of the modern right-to-die movement is relatively objective and highly informative. Many of the ethical issues surrounding the debate are also discussed.

Linda L. Emanual, ed., *Regulating How We Die: The Ethical, Medical, and Legal Issues Surrounding Physician-Assisted Suicide.* Cambridge, MA: Harvard University Press, 1998. In this collection of essays, prominent bioethicists debate euthanasia from moral, legal, and medical perspectives.

Herbert Hendin, *Seduced by Death: Doctors, Patients, and the Dutch Cure.* New York: W.W. Norton, 1997. The author opposes euthanasia and believes that requests to die are caused by depression. He describes euthanasia in the Netherlands and contends that Dutch doctors often ignore guidelines and perform euthanasia when it is inappropriate.

Derek Humphry, *Final Exit: The Practicalities of Self-Deliverance and Assisted Suicide for the Dying.* Eugene, OR: Hemlock Society, 1991. The surprise success of this how-to book on suicide drew much attention to the right-to-die movement. However, the book consists mainly of medical details about potentially lethal drugs rather than arguments for why assisted suicide should be condoned.

Derek Humphry and Mary Clement, *Freedom to Die: People, Politics, and the Right-to-Die Movement.* New York: St. Martin's, 1998. This book is designed as a history of the right-to-die movement, but the authors are right-to-die activists and the book serves as a comprehensive summary of the arguments for both active, voluntary euthanasia and physician-assisted suicide.

Stephen Jamison, *Final Acts of Love: Families, Friends, and Assisted Dying.* New York: G.P. Putnam's Sons, 1995. The author supports euthanasia and intends this book as a guide for determining when it may be appropriate to help a loved one to die.

Gerald A. Larue, *Playing God: Fifty Religions' Views on Your Right to Die.* Wakefield, RI: Moyer Bell, 1996. Most of this book is devoted to an analysis of various religions' views on mercy killing. The author supports physician-assisted dying, however, and the introduction is an informative rebuttal to the major arguments against euthanasia.

Timothy E. Quill, *Death and Dignity: Making Choices and Taking Charge*. New York: W.W. Norton, 1993. Quill recounts the famous case of Diane, a patient whose suicide he assisted. He also discusses the importance of hospice care and provides a detailed proposal to legalize physician-assisted suicide.

Peter Singer, *Rethinking Life and Death: The Collapse of Our Traditional Ethics*. New York: St. Martin's, 1995. In this controversial book, bioethicist Peter Singer argues that traditional morality must be radically altered to include ideas about quality of life, rather than just sanctity of life. In addition to euthanasia, the author addresses medical controversies such as abortion, infanticide, and animal research.

Michael M. Uhlmann, ed., *Last Rights?: Assisted Suicide and Euthanasia Debated*. Grand Rapids, MI: William B. Eerdmans, 1998. This is a valuable collection of original documents pertaining to euthanasia. In addition to several prominent physicians, ethicists, and legal scholars, noted authors include Pope John Paul II, Jack Kevorkian, and the American Medical Association. Excerpts from the court opinions of several recent right-to-die cases are also included.

Periodicals

Pieter V. Admiraal, "Euthanasia in the Netherlands," *Free Inquiry*, Winter 1996/97.

Marcia Angell, "No One Trusts the Dying," *Washington Post*, July 7, 1997.

———, "The Supreme Court and Physician-Assisted Suicide—the Ultimate Right," *New England Journal of Medicine*, January 2, 1997.

Anonymous, "It's Over, Debbie," *Journal of the American Medical Association*, January 8, 1998.

Jay Branegan, "I Want to Draw the Line Myself," *Time*, March 17, 1997.

David R. Carlin Jr., "Microscopic Rights: An Expanding Constitutional Universe," *Commonweal*, June 14, 1996.

William H.A. Carr, "Updating the Physician's Oath," *Saturday Evening Post*, September/October 1995.

Stephen Chapman, "The Dutch Show Where 'Aid-in-Dying' Leads," *Conservative Chronicle*, November 29, 1995.

Death with Dignity Education Center fact sheet, "Misconceptions in the Debate on Death with Dignity," January 1997.

Nicholas Dixon, "On the Difference Between Physician-Assisted Suicide and Active Euthanasia," *Hastings Center Report*, September/October 1998.

Barbara Dority, "'In the Hands of the People': Recent Victories of the Death-with-Dignity Movement," *Humanist*, July/August 1996.

———, "The Ultimate Liberty," *Humanist*, July/August 1997.

Ronald Dworkin et al., "Assisted Suicide: The Philosophers' Brief," *New York Review of Books*, March 27, 1997.

Ezekiel Emanuel, "The Painful Truth About Euthanasia," *Wall Street Journal*, January 7, 1997.

———, "Whose Right to Die?" *Atlantic Monthly*, March 1997.

John C. Fletcher, moderator, "Deciding About Death: Physician-Assisted Suicide and the Courts—a Panel Discussion," *Pharos*, Winter 1998.

Faye J. Girsh, "The Case for Physician Aid in Dying," *Journal of the Hippocratic Society*, Fall 1997.

William Norman Grigg, "Abortion and Beyond," *New American*, January 19, 1998.

John Hardwig, "Is There a Duty to Die?" *Hastings Center Report*, March/April 1997.

Michael Herman, "Assisted Suicide: A History," *Journal of the Hippocratic Society*, Fall 1997.

Yale Kamisar, "It Started with Quinlan: The Ever Expanding 'Right to Die,'" *Los Angeles Times*, March 31, 1996.

———, "The Reasons So Many People Support Physician-Assisted Suicide—and Why These Reasons Are Not Convincing," *Issues in Law & Medicine*, Fall 1996.

Leon R. Kass, "Dehumanization Triumphant," *First Things*, August/September 1996.

Leon R. Kass and Nelson Lund, "Courting Death: Assisted Suicide, Doctors, and the Law," *Commentary*, December 1996.

Jerome P. Kassirer, "The Supreme Court and Physician-Assisted Suicide—the Ultimate Right," *New England Journal of Medicine*, January 2, 1997.

John F. Kavanaugh, "Death's Dignity," *America*, March 8, 1997.

Joe Loconte, "Hospice, Not Hemlock," *Policy Review*, March/April 1998.

Franklin G. Miller et al., "Regulating Physician-Assisted Death," *New England Journal of Medicine*, July 14, 1994.

David Orentlicher, "Navigating the Narrows of Doctor-Assisted Suicide," *Technology Review*, July 1996.

John J. Paris, "Autonomy and Physician-Assisted Suicide," *America*, May 17, 1997.

M. Scott Peck, "Living Is the Mystery," *Newsweek*, March 10, 1997.

Timothy E. Quill, "In the Name of Mercy," *People Weekly*, April 7, 1997.

Wesley J. Smith, "Demanding Death-on-Demand," *Heterodoxy*, May/June 1996.

———, "The Serial Killer as Folk Hero," *Weekly Standard*, July 13, 1998.

John Shelby Spong, "In Defense of Assisted Suicide," *Human Quest*, May/June 1996.

Michael M. Uhlmann, "The Legal Logic of Euthanasia," *First Things*, June/July 1996.

Louis Vernacchio, "Physician-Assisted Suicide: Reflections of a Young Doctor," *America*, August 31, 1996.

Adam Wolfson, "Killing Off the Dying?" *Public Interest*, Spring 1998.

Internet Sources

Burke J. Balch and Randall K. O'Bannon, "Why We Shouldn't Legalize Assisted Suicide, Part I: Suicide and Mental Illness." www.nrlc.org/euthanasia/asisuid1.html.

Robin Bernhoft, "How We Can Win the Compassion Debate," *Citizen Magazine*, June 24, 1996. www.aapainmanage.org/aapm/art1.htm.

Ira Byock, "Why Do We Make Dying So Miserable?" *Washington Post*, January 22, 1997. www.afsp.org/assisted/byock.htm.

Cruzan v. Missouri Department of Health, opinion text. www.soros.org/debate/cruzan.htm.

Thomas J. Gates, "Euthanasia and Assisted Suicide: A Family Practice Perspective," *American Family Physician*, May 15, 1997. www.aafp.org/afp/970515ap/society.html.

Hemlock Society USA, "Hospice and Hemlock: A Position Statement." www2.privatei.com/hemlock/hospice.html.

House Committee on the Judiciary, Subcommittee on the Constitution, *Oversight Hearing: Assisted Suicide in the United States*, 104th Cong., 2nd sess., April 29, 1996. www.house.gov/judiciary/2165.htm.

Derek Humphry, "Why I Believe in Voluntary Euthanasia," February 1995. www.islandnet.com/~deathnet/Humphry_essay.html.

International Anti-Euthanasia Task Force, "Euthanasia: Answers to Frequently Asked Questions." www.iaetf.org/faq.htm.

John Paul II, *Evangelium Vitae (The Gospel of Life)*, March 25, 1995. www.vatican.va/holy_father/john_paul_ii/encyclicals/john-paul-ii_encyclical_25-march-1995_evangelium-vitae_english.html.

Robert D. Lane and Richard Dunstan, "Euthanasia: The Debate Continues," Institute of Practical Philosophy, August 1995. www.mala.bc.ca/www/ipp/euthanas.htm.

Libertarian Party press release, January 9, 1997. www.lp.org/rel/970109-suicide.html.

Diane E. Meier, "A Change of Heart on Assisted Suicide," *New York Times*, April 24, 1998. www.afsp.assisted/meier.htm.

John L. Miller, "Hospice Care or Assisted Suicide: A False Dichotomy," *American Journal of Hospice and Palliative Care*, May/June 1997. http://www2.privatei.com/hemlock/hoscare.html.

National Council on Disability, "Assisted Suicide: A Disability Perspective," March 24, 1997. www.ncd.gov/publications/suicide.html.

National Hospice Organization, "Statement of the National Hospice Organization Opposing the Legalization of Euthanasia and Assisted Suicide," 1997. www.nho.org/pasposition.htm.

Sacred Congregation for the Doctrine of the Faith, "Declaration on Euthanasia," May 5, 1980. http://listserv.american.edu/catholic/church/vatican/cdfeuth.txt.

John Shelby Spong, "On Assisted Suicide: Congressional Testimony," *Voice*, June 1996. www.dfms.org/newark/vox20696.html.

Washington v. Glucksberg, opinion text http://supct.law.cornell.edu/supct/html/96-110.ZO.html.

INDEX

Ninth Circuit Court of Appeals, 41, 42, 67–68

O'Connor, Sandra Day, 34
Oregon, 60–61, 82
  Death with Dignity Act, 19, 79

passive euthanasia, 14–15
  vs. active euthanasia
    distinction between, 39, 40–41
      does not exist, 32–34
    legal necessity of, 40
  as voluntary euthanasia, 14
  see also euthanasia
patients
  autonomy, limits of, 47
  best interests of, 47–49
  depression and, 70–71
  desire assistance in suicide, 54–55
  do not have right to suicide, 65–66
  euthanized without consent, 93
  fear of losing control, 78
  justifiable euthanasia and, 24–25
  legalized euthanasia and
    benefits to, 80–82
    harm to, 71–72, 74–75
  physicians help with death of, 46–47
  physician's responsibility to, 53–54
  power of decisions by, 13, 16, 25, 33–34, 52–53
  right to die, 58–59
    con, 67
  saving life against will of, 12–13
  terminally ill
    vs. disabled, 84–85
    discrimination against, 36–37
    euthanasia limited to, 94
  trust with physicians, 45–46
Peck, M. Scott, 75
physician-assisted suicide
  vs. active euthanasia, 15–16, 93
  humane, 36–37
  is unethical, 45–46, 47
    con, 51
  legality of, 12–13, 54
  legislation on, 19
  vs. passive euthanasia, 42–43
  secretly done, 93, 94
  violates professional integrity, 49
  as voluntary euthanasia, 14, 15

  see also euthanasia
physicians
  cause death of patients, 46–47
  doctrine of double effect and, 80–81
  ethics of, 45–46
  Hippocratic oath and, 52–53
  intentions of, 42
  pain management and, 73–74
  playing God, 47–49
  power of decisions by, 16
  professional integrity of, 49
  refuse suicide for patients, 47
  relief of suffering by, 53, 54–55
  right to kill and, 66–67
  role in euthanasia, 15
  role to relieve suffering, 54–55
Planned Parenthood v. Casey, 68
Prescription Medicide: The Goodness of Planned Death (Kevorkian), 17

Quill, Timothy E., 23, 29, 53, 78
Quinlan, Karen Ann, 11, 13, 14, 33, 41

Rehnquist, William, 42–43
Reinhardt, Stephen, 61
religion, 61
Remmelink Report, 93
right to die
  does not exist, 64–65
  is right to kill, 66–67
  vs. right to suicide, 65–66
right-to-die movement, 11
  compared with Holocaust, 91–92
  on patients' choices, 25
  publicity of, 17–18
  state control and, 60–61
Russell, Bertrand, 11

Sahm, Renee, 22–23
Seneca, 10
Shaw, George Bernard, 11
Smith, Wesley J., 74, 85
Spong, John Shelby, 26, 62
suffering, 61–62
  decision to die and, 78
  patients blamed for, 74–75
  physicians' responsibility to relieve, 53, 54–55
  treatment for, 72–74

ABOUT THE AUTHOR

James Torr is a series editor at Greenhaven Press. He has a degree in biology from Cornell University and has worked as a freelance writer and editor. Originally from Philadelphia, he currently resides in sunny San Diego.